MW00457493

Praise for Jennie Nash's
Build Your Novel from the Inside Out

"This process makes me want to write, and it makes what I'm writing better. I read it before every draft. It's that good."
—**KJ Dell'Antonia**, *New York Times* bestselling author
of *The Chicken Sisters*

"Before anyone is allowed to ask a writer-friend out for coffee 'just to pick your brain' about a book idea, they should be required to read this. It answers SO MANY QUESTIONS. I'm going to keep a stash of copies to hand out."
—**Mary Laura Philpott,** author of
I Miss You When I Blink

"I will sing the praises of the Inside Outline forever. It's f*ing genius."
—**Carla Naumburg**, author of *How to Stop
Losing Your Sh*t With Your Kids*

"Jennie Nash turned me into a plotter and changed the way I think about approaching any new project. I'm an Inside Outside outline fan for life!"
—**Alison Hammer**, author of *You and Me and Us*
and *Little Pieces of Me*

"If you are about to start writing or revising your novel—hold up! You need this book before putting fingers to keyboard. It's a step-by-step design-your-novel manual that encapsulates the most important aspect of great story-telling: how to reach deep into your writerly heart and into the heart of the story you want to bring to life."

— **Janet Fox**, author of *The Artifact Hunters*

"The Inside Outline is making writing easier. I can focus more on the writing rather than discovering what the scene is about when I'm creating it. Why isn't every writer using it? Instead, people are plonking down good money to be told ten key steps in writing dialogue or setting a scene. I'm so grateful I'm no longer one of them."

— **Kate Kimball**, first time novelist

Blueprint for a Nonfiction Book

Plan and Pitch Your Big Idea

JENNIE NASH

Tree Farm Books
Santa Barbara, CA

Blueprint for a Nonfiction Book:
Plan and Pitch Your Big Idea

Copyright © 2022 by Jennie Nash

Tree Farm Books
Santa Barbara, CA
www.jennienash.com

Printed in the United States of America

Library of Congress Control Number: 2022906907

Permission to use material from other works:

Permission to use the table of contents from *The Five Love Languages: How to Express Heartfelt Commitment to your Mate* (Northfield Publishing, January 1, 1992) *by Dr. Gary Chapman* granted by Moody Publishers, Moodypublishers.com.

Permission to use the table of contents from *The Artist's Way: A Spiritual Path to Higher Creativity by Julie Cameron* (Tarcher, January 1, 1992) granted by Penguin Random House LLC.

Author photo by Ashleigh Taylor
Cover design by Stuart Bache
Page layout by Clarity Designworks

ISBN paperback 978-1-7332511-4-3
ISBN ebook 978-1-7332511-5-0

Visit www.jennienash.com/blueprint

Contents

Introduction

At the start of the pandemic, professional speaker and leadership researcher Sara Ross had more than 20 keynote speeches cancelled, and she decided to use the forced downtime to do the thing she had always longed to do: write a book. She hired me as her book coach and during our first meeting said, "I know just what will be in it. I've given this speech a hundred times."

She described to me a poem she loved about falling into holes and finding your way around them the next time you walked down that same road. She often referenced this poem in her talks, which were about the traps high achieving businesspeople tend to fall into over and over again. Her audience connected with the poem as much as she did. She thought she would title her book *Falling in Holes* and structure it according to the six most common traps.

This concept meant a lot to Ross, but it struck me as a bit negative and simplistic. I sensed that Ross had an optimistic outlook about high achieving businesspeople and that she had more to say to them about their relationship to work, beyond avoiding traps.

We worked through the *Blueprint* process—and it turned out that Ross's keynote contained only a tiny fraction of her big idea. Once she realized that a book could contain so much more—that there was room for it, and she didn't have the constraint of 90 minutes on a stage in front of a restless audience—she let herself soar.

By the time she finished crafting her book proposal, her idea was a deep and compelling argument for how people who are passionate about their work can maintain their vitality over the course of their careers. It was a much bigger idea than the one about falling into the same traps—although that idea is certainly part of it. The book she will be publishing has the clever and resonant title, *Dear Work: I Love You, But Something Has to Change.*

In your career, you have no doubt developed a keynote speech or a conference presentation or a podcast interview or a workshop curriculum or a pitch deck that showcases your ideas—but those things are very different from a book. A book is a uniquely powerful way to deliver your big idea to the world. When readers pick a book to read, they are making a commitment to sink into the author's way of thinking. They are prepared to go deep in a way that just doesn't happen in a public or group presentation. We all know the experience of feeling like an author is speaking directly to us, peering into our soul, and articulating something that changes the way we see the world. It's almost akin to falling in love: we feel seen, we feel whole, we feel inspired.

Books that have the power to move us like that are not easy to write. We can be lulled into thinking they are because skilled writers make it *look* easy, but there is no shortcut, no fast and easy success formula, and no way to reverse engineer it. Writing a book is a complex intellectual, creative, and entrepreneurial undertaking and to write a good one, you have to put in the work—and I don't just mean cranking out words. The work that is going to have the most impact is the work you do before you write a single word of the book itself.

You will hear all kinds of advice about the physical act of writing—write every morning, write 1000 words a day—but those habits don't matter if you don't know what you're writing, or why, or for whom.

You will also hear advice about craft—how to make sure you're not using passive phrasing, how to make sure each chapter has narrative drive—but craft is the frosting on the cake. You first need to bake the cake.

I developed the *Blueprint* method because the experts, executives, educators, and entrepreneurs who were coming to me for help with their books couldn't answer the most fundamental questions about their projects. People who would never start a business without understanding their customer had not thought about their ideal reader in a strategic way. People who would never launch a product without market testing it had not bothered to look at what other books were on the shelf.

I needed a way to help these writers answer the fundamental questions about their book, their ideal reader, and their content before they started to try to write. I wanted a tool that would lead directly to the book proposal so that they could focus on the task of selling their project. I hoped that it would all lead to a more seamless development process and a more powerful pitch.

The *Blueprint for a Book* System

The *Blueprint for a Nonfiction Book* system walks you through 14 foundational questions. It is divided into three parts—Part 1: Understand Your Book Fundamentals; Part 2: Get to Know Your Ideal Reader; Part 3: Design a Structure.

Some of the questions may seem simple and obvious, but they are not meant to be answered quickly. You're not checking off boxes on a government form—*check, yes, got it, next.* Every step you take in the *Blueprint* has the potential to enrich and impact the earlier steps, so it's not a linear, straightforward process. You will repeatedly adjust your answers to make them clearer, stronger, and more solid. So, you revise and edit. You tweak and trim. You go back through the steps until your logic is sound, your argument is solid, your voice is clear, and you have a plan for a book that will inform, instruct, or inspire.

Once your *Blueprint* is finished, the next step on the path to publication is to use the material you've developed to create a book proposal. I walk you through the development of a book proposal in Part 4.

In Part 5, I explain what you need to do to pitch your proposal to literary agents, which is how you land a book deal with a traditional publishing house.

Your Path to Publishing

Traditional publishing is just one way to get a book into readers' hands. There are many other paths to publishing. The book you are holding in your hands, for example, is one that I published independently. Some of my clients work with hybrid publishers—which means that the author works with a publishing team but shoulders some of the upfront financial risk and stands to earn more on the backend. Tomorrow, there could be some new way of publishing books that none of us has ever heard of.

The work you do in the *Blueprint* prepares you for any publishing path because it forces you to think fully about your idea, your reader, the book's structure, and your plan for connecting with readers. That being said, I'm going to assume that you want to pitch a book proposal to an agent and try for a traditional publishing deal, and here's why I am making that assumption: the work you have to do to achieve that goal sets a high bar for excellence. It is an effective strategy no matter how you eventually publish.

- A writer who wishes to land an agent and a traditional publishing deal must have a book proposal. This is also true for most academic presses and mid-tier publishers, not just the Big Five.

- A writer working with a hybrid publisher usually needs to have a book proposal. Some hybrid publishers will help writers develop them, but a proposal is where the book development process starts.

- A writer publishing independently will benefit greatly from a book proposal. You don't need it to convince anyone to invest in your project, but you need it to organize your thoughts to make good publishing decisions.

It's Time to Get Real

The *Blueprint* method is equally effective for people who think they know exactly what they want to write, people who have ideas that are half-baked, and people who are noodling several different ideas and not sure which direction to go. It can even work for people with first drafts that are ready for revision. All you need to take advantage of the *Blueprint* is a book idea you want to share with the world, an audience you hope to reach, and the willingness to figure out the best way to pin that idea to the page.

I love coaching people through the *Blueprint* because it is where ideas become real. It's where vague "I want to write a book someday" sentiments turn into "I love this book and I am writing it" proclamations. Dreaming of writing a book is all well and good but taking effective action towards your dreams is even better.

You can download a workbook to capture your answers to the *Blueprint* questions and a book proposal template at www.jennienash.com/blueprint.

Note: The examples I share in this book are examples from my clients and, in some cases, the clients of Author Accelerator certified book coaches—all of whom I personally thank in the acknowledgements. These writers are sharing some of the first words they ever wrote about their books, when their ideas were new and fragile, and when they were still shaky and unsure about what they were doing. I encourage all my clients to be as raw and real as they possibly can because that's how you get to something that is going to feel alive and authentic on the page. It can look pretty rough at the start. I have left all examples exactly as they came into me as a reminder that this process is iterative. Please be gracious in your reading of them.

PART 1

Book Fundamentals

The fundamental elements of a book are the core aspects of the idea itself and the deep-level motivation that the author brings to the project. These elements are often overlooked by writers eager to get words on the page, get to "the end," and get their book into the world, but skipping them is dangerous. It leads to manuscripts that never make it off the desktop, books that fall flat, and authors who don't make the kind of impact they want to make. Spending time getting clear on the fundamental elements is the first—and most important—step in turning your vague idea into a big idea.

Why Write This Book?

When I ask my clients why they want to write a book, they will often start by giving a simple answer: "I want to share what I have learned" or "I don't want other people to suffer like I did." These answers are part of the truth, but they often shield deeper reasons. These reasons, this deeper why, form the core of your motivation and momentum; you'll draw on these reasons when you feel despair or imposter syndrome.

If you never ask yourself why you are writing, you are far more likely to write in circles, fall into frustration and doubt, and come to believe that writing depends on some elusive muse or a series of special habits (e.g., write 1500 words a day, write for an hour every day, write when the full moon is waning) rather than deep self-reflection, discipline, and persistence.

Identifying your why first has an enormous impact on your capacity to both write and complete a book that resonates with your desired reader. It's often the difference between writing a book that people want to read and either a.) never finishing, or b.) finishing, but writing something that is so watered down and wishy-washy that it fails to make an impact.

You can write your way to an answer—absolutely. I have done it, and writers I know have done it, and we have all heard of famous writers who have done it, but the truth is that for most of us most of the time, it's wildly inefficient, ineffective, painful, and unnecessary. That's why we start with why.

Why Yes, I'm Referencing Simon Sinek

You've probably read Simon Sinek's mega-selling business book, *Start With Why*, or seen the TED Talk. His message is crystal clear and powerful: "People don't buy what you do; people buy why you do it." In other words, it's not enough to create a product that people might want to buy or a book that readers might want to read. Your story has to spring from a deep conviction on your part, or it risks not resonating with the readers you want to captivate.

So all this work you're going to do in the *Blueprint* on what your book will be hinges on *why* you want to write it— on why it is haunting you, or why you care. If you can articulate that, it will give your story all kinds of power.

Your External Why

Let's start with the external reasons why you want to write a book—things you believe writing a book will get you in the world. These are probably connected to the return on investment (ROI) of your time, energy, and money.

At the top of most people's list is the desire to be recognized more broadly for their expertise. Writing a book is about becoming seen and heard. Different people have different concepts of what recognition and validation look like. It might be that you are quoted in the publication of record for your field or offered a column there. It might be that you are invited to speak at a prestigious event. It might be that the people you admire in the field come to admire you.

Many people hope that writing a book will make them a lot of money in book sales, and it might. You could receive a $25,000 advance from a traditional publisher or a $150,000 advance or a $1,000,000 advance, and then you will receive 15 percent royalties on every book sold once that advance earns out.

Or you could work with a hybrid publisher, which requires an upfront investment from the author, and make even more money on the backend.

Michael Bungay Stanier's business management book, *The Coaching Habit: Say Less, Ask More & Change the Way You Lead Forever* (published by Page Two Books), has sold more than a million copies. He makes between $4 and $6 per book, plus the book drives business and revenue for his consulting firm. That all adds up to a robust return on the investment of writing a book.

Most people, in truth, don't earn anywhere near that much money. The *New York Times* reported in 2020 that 98 percent of books sold fewer than 5,000 copies. This reality means that writing a book might not be a great financial bet if you rely solely on book sales to earn out your investment of time and effort. "The majority of writers don't earn a living from book sales alone," writes Jane Friedman in *The Business of Being a Writer*, "People don't go into the writing profession for the big bucks unless they're delusional."

So why bother?

Because of the possibility of making an impact and extending your reach. My client Jenn Lim, author of *Beyond Happiness: How Authentic Leaders Prioritize Purpose and People for Growth and Impact*, a *Wall Street Journal* bestseller, introduced me to the idea of what she calls "the other ROI"—meaning ripples of impact. Lim's book is about finding purpose in the workplace and living that purpose every day. The ripples of impact happen when you connect with fellow humans in an authentic way. Writing a book gives you a way to make an impact and spread your ideas far and wide. This often leads to lucrative consulting or speaking gigs, the opportunity to collaborate on interesting projects and initiatives, and the chance to be part of powerful conversations.

Here's how Michael Bungay Stanier puts it: "We've all seen our marketing heroes grow a base of fans, then customers, then empires through 'content marketing.' And the big kahuna in content marketing is the book. This is how you officially rise to 'Thought Leader' status, it's how you differentiate yourself from your competitors, you drive revenue, you launch your speaking career, you start hanging out with other cool authors."

Thought leaders definitely hang out with each other. I love to listen to podcasts about business, personal growth, and creativity, and I am often struck by how all the authors at a certain level know each other and boost each other's work. Adam Grant appears on Brené Brown's podcast when his new book comes out, and Brené Brown appears on Grant's podcast when her new book comes out, and then you see that they both have been on Guy Raz's show and you start to notice that Indra Nooyi is in all the same places talking about her new book, too. All these thought leaders know each other and read each other's work and promote each other's work to their massive audiences. These are ripples of impact at a high level, but even at less stratospheric heights, the ripples work the same way, and they can be profound.

Here are what the ripples of impact can look like:

- You attract followers who are interested in hearing more of what you have to say, expanding your ability to influence, educate, illuminate, comfort, or entertain people.

- You attract the attention of traditional media when they are looking for experts to quote in your industry.

- You attract the attention of podcasters and radio and TV producers.

- You receive invitations to speak at industry events and at events outside of your field.

- You can easily share your most powerful content with key audiences.

- You have reason to connect with other influencers—to strike up a conversation, collaborate, and connect with each other's audience.

- You have the chance to build a legacy around your thinking.

These are the reasons people invest the time, energy, and money in writing books—and some of these outcomes come with financial rewards far greater than the book itself.

It's important to identify your external why for writing a book, but there is another layer of motivation to understand as well.

Your Internal Why

The internal reasons people write are the ones that tend to sustain them through the roadblocks and challenges of a long development process. These reasons often come from a place of rage or injustice, which could be a simple jealousy, a different way of looking at things than the prevailing wisdom, or a deep-rooted sense of social justice. Often people who have something to say are saying it in opposition to something else—some other idea, or social movement, or injustice, or prevailing belief, or experience they've had.

At the end of the day, writing is all about raising your voice and staking your claim. You speak your truth, claim your authority, take a stand for what you believe in. We can talk all day long about how to write—both the craft of it and the practice of it—but the hardest part by far is stepping into your power.

I have the great privilege of working with people who are very accomplished in their fields—entrepreneurs and executives and thought leaders—and every single one of them rubs up against the difficulty of raising their voice. Will people care? Do I have the right to tell this story? Is it good enough? Will it matter? These are not only questions the beginner asks; these are questions every writer asks. And they are questions about raising one's voice.

The way to answer these questions and combat the doubt that comes with them is to connect to your why. Tap into your motivation, the reason you care, your rage, and your passion. That is how you find your voice and how you finish your book.

CASE STUDY #1
Why write this book? by Dr. Jennifer Noble

I must write this book because I am getting tired. I am getting tired of how insulated Mainstream White America is from the rest of America (and really the world), and how insulated middle- and upper-income America is from anyone who makes less. It seems that the prevailing belief about how to be a "good parent" (or perhaps to raise "successful" children) is to first have money. Somehow money has been the way to create the environment that will allow children to thrive. There is a strong classist view that anyone who makes below a certain amount is inherently inferior, thus money should automatically make one superior. If children need safety, buy a big enough house in a "safe" neighborhood—don't worry about the emotional safety and security that should be fostered within your family. If children need enriching activities—spend the money to put them in all the extracurricular activities (especially those that will make them competitive for university)—don't worry about filling their days with so much "enrichment" that they are exhausted and riddled with anxiety because they have no time to think their own thoughts. Drawing at home on scrap paper? No! "Creative Drawing Art Camp" for $3,000 over 3 weeks? Yes! Spend the money for the good schools. $15k per year for kindergarten is OK and maybe necessary, family dinner together is not! Parents are working nonstop to buy all the gadgets. They are preoccupied with whether they have enough money to get their kids to UCLA or USC (meeting someone's bar of success). If they get tired or feel overwhelmed, they can feel momentary satisfaction that their kid has had a better life than "the poor" families— right before the anxiety of possibly falling into poverty if they don't work hard enough kicks in again.

I am also tired of parenting advice that is only based on WEIRD cultures (Western Educated Industrialized Rich Democratic). Each book presenting the newest advice still assumes a higher income, suburban neighborhood, and

Euro-American culture and values. This is such a blind spot that families who do not fit this description are judged for their parenting and taught to believe that the only way to "correct" their parenting mistakes is to adopt this WEIRD stance to parenting.

So, I guess I am tired of erasure. There are so many non-Western/non-Euro-American, less educated, underprivileged, poor families who raise their children down the street from the most sought-after neighborhoods and school districts and their children are successful! Those parents aren't reading all the parenting books. They aren't searching the parenting blogs, they aren't fighting to get an interview at the best preschool in the county. They are living where they can afford to live, creating as much safety in their home as they can and using a style of parenting that utilizes multiple generations of knowledge and a community of people to help their child be successful. They're parenting is not driven by what they can afford to provide (although they feel this same pressure), but what they hope to instill.

I say erasure because, no one turns to a low-income family of color to see what they can learn from them. No one asks, what can we learn from these "poor, inferior" families? If there is any attention at all, it seems to be more out of pity and awe about how they must be "so strong" to endure "so much hardship," rather than a deeper look at family interactions or parent lessons that all would benefit from adopting. Instead, the WEIRD parents teach their kids fear of lower income families, fear of families of color (assumed to be low income), they teach that money is the main thing that separates and proves their success and thus superiority. Then we wonder why kids of those parents are shocked to see lower income students of color next to them in their private high schools or USC classes and assume (because they had less money) there must be some other explanation for how they got in and doubt they will be able to make it to graduation.

I want to challenge this thought that more money equals better parenting. I want to force others to really see the lower income people of color who are working right next to them—in their homes, in their businesses, in their schools and restaurants. I want to force families to think about who they would be were it not for their income level. Could they still find a sense of identity were it not tied to how expensive their schools were or how much their home is worth? More importantly, can their children understand who they are without it being deeply tied to and defined by their family status?

"Working hard" vs. "the struggle"—the first is an American value, the other is an American shame.

CASE STUDY #2
Why write this book? by Andrea Jarrell

In *The War of Art*, Steven Pressfield describes the unlived life so many of us long for—that coulda, shoulda, woulda life we see as our true calling if we just had the courage to go after it. To live the life I wanted, I spent years defeating my resistance. No regrets. No sitting on the sidelines. I told myself, *live so you're not afraid of dying*. Yet, it wasn't until I hit my late fifties that I understood dying wasn't what I was afraid of.

My girlhood dreams had covered college, moving to New York, traveling the world, writing books, falling in love, getting married, having children, financial and professional success. I'd done all of that. Traditionally, in one's fifties you're meant to start the ride down, coasting on whatever success you've earned by then. But from my perspective, it had taken me too long to become the person I wanted to be. How could I have finally kicked "the resistance" only to be told my time was up? Yet for the first time in a long time, I didn't know how to grow and that scared me. I'd never looked to anyone in their sixties and seventies and thought *Ooh, I want to do that*! I had never been taught to dream about life beyond age 50 or so.

My grandmother spent her fifties running from aging: divorce, new marriage, travel, facelift. But at the age of 59, she was still afraid. She began to drink more—a lot more. One night, she passed out and drowned in her bathtub. It's not that my mother and I think she meant to do it. Not really. But we both believe that some part of her just couldn't face turning 60.

Now, on the brink of turning 60 myself, I believe the challenge isn't how to live so you aren't afraid of dying. The challenge is to live so you aren't afraid of going on, of getting older—of not being young. My grandmother gave up. She saw only two choices: deny (pretend aging isn't happening, deny its value) or decline (accept that older means a diminished life and that you have no real currency left in the world). All around me, I see my middle-aged peers trapped by the same choices: decline or deny.

I [am writing] this book because I needed to find a new way to be older. I thought there had to be more options than deny or decline. My ambition was to "reinvent aging." But how could I prove to myself and to others that this was more than a fantasy? I needed new role models, so I went looking for them. What I found was a revolution. What I found was a third way in which I was no longer afraid to get older. I truly believe that it is never too late to live the unlived life that calls to us. But I also know that it's a constant choice we must keep making. I [have] to write this book to teach myself what the third way looks like and to find the courage to take it.

TAKE ACTION

- Write one page on why you must write this book. What is your external why? What do you hope to get from it?

  ☐ To make money

  ☐ To make a name for myself as an expert/authority

  ☐ To influence/educate/illuminate/comfort/entertain people

  ☐ To raise my voice/speak up/claim my story

  ☐ To prove that I can do it, either to myself or others

  ☐ Because I feel called to do it/I am burning to do it/I can't rest until I do it

  ☐ To leave a legacy for my family

  ☐ To model for my kids what it means to pursue a dream (hard work, frustration, failure, perseverance, etc.)

  ☐ Other:

- What is your internal why for writing this book? What does it mean to you on a deeply personal level?

....

Why Are You the Best Person to Write This Book?

You won't find the answer to this step on your resume. Your answer might include accomplishments and accolades if those things provide evidence that you have the knowledge you need to write the book you are envisioning. The real question we want to answer here is, why do you believe yourself to be the authority on this topic? Not what the world says—what *you* say.

Your answer probably has a lot to do with the reason you wrote in the previous step for why you care about this idea— what motivates you, what you are passionate about, why you want to be heard.

It might have to do with what you think about all the other people who have written on this topic and how they have approached it.

It might have to do with a particular way you have of looking at a topic. I once had a client who had spent a lifetime studying Bob Dylan. He knew the fan sites, every book ever written, the concert schedule, the big anniversaries. He wrote a quirky, inspiring book about his idol. He was the best person to write his book simply because of his obsession—and you would have found nothing about that on his resume.

You might be the best person to write this book because of something that is happening in the world right now. Maybe you experienced something unique or are in a unique position to report or observe on a trend.

There can be a thousand books about the same topic, but no one can write the book that you can. No one brings the same set of experiences and beliefs that you do. No one has the same perspective and the same voice.

> **PRO TIP:** *What if you might not be the best person to write this book? If this question comes up for you, write about that doubt. One of the best ways to do this is to write a nightmare book review—the worst thing you can imagine people saying about your book. Write something that would really sting—"Who is this privileged white woman to be talking about her problems when the world is falling apart?" "Who is this guy to be telling people what to do in business when his company only makes $2M a year?" You can counteract the criticism as you develop your book.*

CASE STUDY #1
Why are you the best person to write this book?
by Michael Melcher

Everyone deserves a chance to be successful. But not everyone has the same chance of success, and the path to success is often murky. Millions of people fall short of their career ambitions not because they aren't trying but because they don't know the unwritten rules and secret codes for getting the most out of their careers.

This problem particularly afflicts people who are the first—first to go to college, first to go into a particular career, first to enter an inner sanctum of elitism. When you are first, you will face key decisions that will determine your long-term success but no one from your family or community can tell you what to do. So how do you figure this out?

The reason I must write this book is that I know what to do. I know what the secrets are. I know what competencies matter, how you figure out authentic as opposed to conventional success, how you build powerful networks and how you can communicate in a powerful way. These practices are not widely known but they are learnable.

I have spent the past 20 years working with a huge range of people—including people who grew up poor, people who are ethnic minorities, people who are immigrants or from immigrant families, people who are firsts—to help them get what they want out of their careers. Most of my clients are (1) in or trying to get into elite companies or organizations and (2) stuck in some way, either not sure how to get ahead, how to get better at certain things, or how to have the life they want. Every single one of my clients has made progress, in many cases life changing. The coaching work we do doesn't transfer anything from me to them but rather helps them unlock what is already possible. There are only so many people I'm ever going to work with directly. I want to bring these lessons to a bigger audience.

More attention than ever is being paid to the experiences of less privileged people, yet currently it focuses almost entirely on "systemic" problems. Ironically, this leads to a determination that less privileged people—including firsts—can't succeed until the system itself changes. This burns me up because there is a LOT individuals can do to have the career they want, and I will tell them what it is. I don't want anyone to wait until the revolution comes to have the success they deserve. There's a lot you can do RIGHT NOW.

CASE STUDY #2
Why are you the best person to write this book?
by Becky Vieira

In the beginning, I didn't realize I had PPD [post-partum depression] because none of my symptoms were on the checklist written inside the measly hospital brochure I was sent home with. What I didn't know is that it manifests differently for every mother, it can change and evolve. I knew I loved my son and wanted to protect him, but I wasn't in love with him. I didn't enjoy motherhood and worried I'd made a mistake. I also began experiencing bouts of rage, never toward my child or myself, that I would take out on my kitchen walls or dishes. This further fed the lies my brain was telling me, that I was a bad mother and didn't deserve my son.

This was the side of motherhood no one told me about, the one that left me feeling guilty and ashamed. I was convinced at this point that if I asked for help and revealed my true thoughts and actions that I would be committed or lose custody of my son. I stayed silent and continued suffering, which led me toward plans of running away and taking my own life.

Social media has helped to close the gap between available information and reality to some extent. I have been sharing my motherhood story, my "what it's really like" collection of truths, and the response has been overwhelmingly positive. People have been asking for more. Women are craving the real, the ugly, and the inside out of motherhood, one that is rooted in reality and not a best-case scenario overview. Whether it be to prepare them for what's to come or make them feel less alone in what they've endured, the days of staying silent in our struggle need to end. I've been able to share this in piecemeal form, but the starts and stops created by doling this out in the form of separate social media posts leaves a lot to be desired. I believe we need a complete collection of what the first year of motherhood truly looks like.

I want to be part of the change in how society approaches women and motherhood. I want to see more acceptance of moms, more support and help. Ultimately, I'd like to play a role in created increased support for maternal mental health, raising awareness for PPD especially and bringing it to the attention of our government. When we are able to make national changes to the mental health support of mothers I want to be there. I want to share my story before congress when they are evaluating and analyzing the needs of a bill to support new mothers.

TAKE ACTION

- Write no more than a page about why you are the best person to write this book.

....
What's Your Point?

Now that you've established why you care about this idea and why you are the best person to write it, we can turn our focus to the point you want the book to make. The point of the book is different than the idea itself. The idea of Gretchen Rubin's *The Happiness Project*, for example, is to chronicle a year spent consciously trying to be happier but the point is that you can, in fact, become happier by changing both small and large habits. The idea is connected to structure, which we'll get to in a minute. For now, let's just focus on the point.

Every book is, at heart, an argument for something—for a belief, a way of life, a vision of the future, a way to solve a problem, a way to make a friend, or fall in love, or raise a child or connect with your soul. The point is that message. It's the belief and understanding your reader will have when they finish reading your book.

Don't be alarmed if your point sounds like a bumper sticker. There are a vast number of books that can be told with the point, "Small habits lead to big results," or "Children need time to play and explore" or "Leadership is about adhering to core values in times of chaos." When you can frame your idea as a cliché, it means you're getting down to a universal idea that everyone understands. You will make it distinctive through structure, shape, and voice, so there's no need to worry now about it being obvious.

I often ask writers who are stuck at this stage of the process to imagine that they are giving a TED Talk. They have 18 minutes and they can only make one point, one argument. What is it going to be? If giving a TED talk doesn't inspire you, imagine yourself with Oprah on Super Soul Sunday or on the front page of the *Harvard Business Review* or *Rolling Stone*— whatever place or publication that would be the pinnacle of success for your area of expertise. What's the headline on the magazine cover? What does Oprah say when she introduces you?

It is not unusual for a writer to change their point as they write forward and get deeper into the work. That's fine; it's far better to have to revise or tweak your point than not to have one at all.

CASE STUDY
What's the Point?

Here is a list of the point of some nonfiction books you are probably familiar with. Note that these are my ideas about the points of these books, not the authors' ideas:

- *Made to Stick* by Chip Heath and Dan Heath argues that every company is in the business of telling stories.

- *Big Magic* by Elizabeth Gilbert proves that everyone possesses the power to be creative.

- *The Gift of Failure* by Jessica Lahey argues that the high-pressure culture of achievement is toxic to kids.

- *Strengths Finder 2.0* by Tom Rath argues that it's more powerful to focus on your strengths than your weaknesses.

- *Grain Brain* by David Perlmutter, MD argues that carbs are bad for your brain.

- *The Happiness Project* by Gretchen Rubin shows that changing small habits can lead to a happier life.

- *The Tipping Point* by Malcolm Gladwell proves that ideas spread like epidemics.

TAKE ACTION

- What's the point of your book? Just write it out—there's no need to make it sound snazzy at this stage.

Where Will Your Book Sit on the Shelf?

Imagine your book is finished, published, and out in the world. You walk into a bookstore. Where will you find your book?

This might be the easiest question you've ever been asked. Is it a book about backpacking in Australia? A cookbook based on your mother's famous curry? A book about how to get your personal finances in order? The answer about where the book sits might be very obvious. These books belong firmly in one category: travel, cooking, personal finance.

But what if the backpacking book is really a book about being a digital nomad in the land down under? What if the point is not about travel but about living a certain kind of entrepreneurial lifestyle? Would the book be more at home on a business bookshelf?

What if the cookbook is really about growing your own herbs and spices? What if the point is that gardening is the secret of making curry? Would it be more logical to place it in the gardening section of the bookstore?

What if the personal finance book is aimed at helping elderly couples prepare for death? That book might be found on a very different bookshelf than a book aimed at helping college graduates step into the working world. A book can't be everything to everyone or it will end up speaking to no one.

Writers frequently object to this question. They don't like to choose. They argue that their book is both a cookbook *and* a gardening book; that it's great for people who want to backpack around Australia to see the country *and* for entrepreneurs who want to work from the road. Books often have multiple identities—this is part of what makes them rich and resonant for the reader. But to position the book to sell, it has to have one shelf where it belongs. Books are sold based on category; the bookseller or the librarian must know exactly where to put it. You have to choose.

It can help to go to an actual bookstore when you're making this decision and to look at online bookstores to research different categories.

TAKE ACTION

- Describe where you will find your book in the bookstore.

Choose a Working Title

Choosing a working title for your project is one of the most powerful ways to define it. A good title can help you hone your concept. It can also help you:

- **Focus on your purpose and your point.** I heard Jay Shetty (on Guy Raz's podcast) point out that the title of his book was *Think Like a Monk*, not *Live Like a Monk*. He is not suggesting that we all give up our worldly possessions and get up at 4 a.m. to pray. He is suggesting that we can train our minds for peace and purpose. His title is making his point and showing the promise of what we can expect from the book.

- **Zero in on your ideal reader.** *Rachel Rodgers'* company is called Hello Seven (which is about earning seven figures), and I imagine she considered that as a book title. It is, after all, a catchy phrase that speaks to her expertise about helping people build wealth based on their intellectual property. But she titled her book, *We Should All Be Millionaires: A Woman's Guide to Earning More, Building Wealth, and Gaining Economic Power.* This is a powerful title because she is speaking directly to her core audience (women) about her core idea (the fact that money can create systemic change as well as individual earning power).

- **Set a tone.** Authors Rory Freedman and Kim Barnouin wanted to write a book about the vegan lifestyle. It would have been easy to choose a title with the word vegan in it and to write about eating a plant-based diet in a straightforward way. But the authors were not interested in straightforward; they were on a mission. "We wanted to start a dialogue," Barnouin told Bizwomen—and they succeeded. Their book became a cultural phenomenon that sold many millions of copies. It's a provocative title: *Skinny Bitch: A No-Nonsense, Tough-Love Guide for Savvy Girls Who Want to Stop Eating Crap and Start Looking Fabulous!*

When you're brainstorming titles, be sure to consider subtitles, too. Subtitles perform several important functions: they give context for the title, they amplify the point of the book, and they give you a way to optimize for online searches by using keywords.

If the main title is short and catchy but vague, the subtitle can do the heavy lifting of explaining what the book is about. A title like *Quiet* by Susan Cain, for example, doesn't mean a lot until you see the subtitle: *The Power of Introverts in a World That Can't Stop Talking.*

The Emperor of All Maladies by Siddhartha Mukherjee gets your attention and the subtitle—*A Biography of Cancer*—provides the context, an explanation, and a hint as to the structure of the book.

Your title could change a hundred times, and your publisher may have the final say on what goes on the cover, but it's good to start with a working title that can serve as your North Star as you write.

To find a good working title, start by brainstorming a list of 10 ideas.

> **PRO TIP:** *If you get stuck developing a list of titles, try one of these constraints to spur your thinking:*
> - One word (*Flow, Outliers, Caste, Blink*).
> - Six words (Six words is Hemingway's famous "shortest short story" concept—a brilliant way into a title simply because it offers a constraint rather than letting you be totally free to wander around the vast universe of your mind. *The Summer of Beer and Whiskey; A Heartbreaking Work of Staggering Genius*).
> - A title that includes a number (*The 4-Hour Workweek; The $100 Startup*).
> - A title with imagery/metaphor/symbols (*Who Moved My Cheese?; Swim with the Sharks*).
> - Fill in the blanks: *The (adjective) (noun)*. (*The Artist's Way; The War of Art*).
> - A list (*Eat, Pray, Love; Women, Food and God; Gödel, Escher, Bach*).

Zero in on your favorites and start playing around with title + subtitle combinations. Remember to think about the sound of the title, and the rhythm of it, and not just the meaning. A title that is catchy or melodic will be easier to remember than one that isn't.

It can be smart to ask a few friends what they think of your top title candidates, or even to go out to your followers to ask them to vote. It's a fun way to get people engaged with your ideas and to let them know that you are working on a book.

CASE STUDY #1
Title brainstorm for a book about the first year of motherhood by Becky Vieria

1. *You're Not the Only One: When Motherhood Feels Uglier Than It Should*

2. *You're Not the Only One: Diapers, Tears, Depression and Other Real Truths About the First Year of Motherhood*

3. *All Moms Feel Like Failures: Surviving the First Year of Motherhood*

4. *The Sh*t No One Tells You About Motherhood* (I like this concept, but this isn't the right way to say it)

5. *What Your Friends Should Have Told You*

6. *Motherhood is Hard. This Book Will Help* (this is kind of the gist of what I want to say)

7. *It's Normal To Cry in Motherhood*

8. *The Formerly Miserable Mom's Guide To Enjoying the First Year of Motherhood* (I like this one the best because I feel like it encapsulates everything I want to say. I was a miserable mom, that's true. I'm not anymore, and I want to share what I've learned so no one else is miserable like I was.)

9. *The Bullshit-Free First Year of Motherhood*

10. *What No One Told Me: A Real Look at New Motherhood*

11. *Normalizing Motherhood*

12. *You're Not Alone: The Unfiltered First Year of Motherhood*

13. *Everyone's Been Lying To You: Motherhood is Harder Than You Think (And better, too)*

Becky played around with this list and decided this combination was her favorite:

The Ultimate Guide for First-Time Moms to Make Sure They Are Okay, Too

It seemed to me that this title was a little clunky and that instead of hitting on the idea itself, it was only circling around it. I asked Becky to explain why she liked the title and she said, "People need to understand the baby will be just fine. We need to make sure the moms are okay, too."

We both heard a new title idea in those words: *The Baby Will Be Just Fine.*

Becky liked the concept of guide, however, and wanted to keep that in the title. She also talked about the reality that her ideal reader often feels guilty for spending time and energy on themselves when they have an infant to care for. She came up with title + subtitle combination:

The Baby Will Be Just Fine: The Selfish Mom's Guide to Surviving the First Year

She loved this title and immediately saw a way to clarify it and make it even stronger. She added just two words:

*The Baby Will Be Just Fine: The (**Not So**) Selfish Mom's Guide to Surviving the First Year*

This title is memorable and rhythmic. It's also funny and it perfectly states the point of Becky's book.

CASE STUDY #2
Title brainstorm for a book about parenting, money, and class by Jennifer Noble

1. *Money is ruining the American family*

2. *Lessons from poverty: parenting secrets from families we ignore*

3. *The Millionaire Family*

4. *What the Millionaire Family is Missing*

5. *Rich Family, Poor Family: What the poor do in their parenting that rich families do not*

6. *The Money Focused Parent*

7. *The Status Focused Parent?*

8. *The Poor Family's Secret to Raising Successful Kids*

9. *Mo Money, Mo Problems: What Low Income Parents Teach their children that Rich Families Don't*

10. *The Accidentally Classist Parent*

11. *The Unwittingly Classist Parent*

12. *Crumbs from the Poor Man's Table* (play on crumbs from the rich man's table)

13. *Food from the Poor Man's Table*

14. *The Poor Man's Parenting Secrets*

15. *Anti-Entitlement: Parenting Secrets from Low Income Parents*

16. *Entitlement, Classism and the Child with an Unexamined Identity*

17. *Parenting on the Other Side of the Tracks*

18. *The Secrets of Parenting from the Other Side of the Tracks*

19. *The Invisible Family: How Low-Income Minority Parents Raise Successful Children*

Jennifer liked *The Secrets of Parenting from the Other Side of the Tracks*. It put a positive spin on the idea she wanted to write about and had a counterintuitive nature to it that would get people's attention. The only problem was that it was a little tough to say—it felt like a lot of words. That's where a subtitle can do some of the work. She could shift the word "parenting" or the concept of parenting to the subtitle. That meant her title could be the very elegant:

Secrets from the Other Side of the Tracks

The work was then to develop a subtitle that captured the point of the book, mentioned the idea of parenting, and said something about the promise the book would offer. After playing around, Jennifer came up with this combination:

Secrets from the Other Side of the Tracks: What Poor Minority Kids Can Teach Your Kids About Changing the World

This title is powerful and memorable title. It served as a guiding light to Jennifer as she developed her book.

TAKE ACTION

- Brainstorm a list of at least 10 title + subtitle ideas.
- Play around with different combinations to see what feels resonant and powerful.
- Bring in trusted friends or followers to get outside perspective.
- Choose a working title and as you work on other elements of the *Blueprint*, keep returning to it to see if you can improve upon it.

PART 2

. . . . . .

Get To Know
Your Ideal Reader

After working through the story fundamentals in Part 1, you probably have a vague idea about your ideal reader—but a vague idea is not good enough. A book is a commercial product that you want people (agents and publishers) to invest in and consumers (readers) to buy. Just like any other commercial product, you have to be clear about who it's for and why they might care.

Is your parenting book for soccer moms? There are soccer moms who want their first grader to play because the kid spends too much time playing video games and soccer moms who are banking on their high school junior getting a college scholarship. Which reader are you speaking to?

Is your career coaching book for people changing careers in midlife? There are workers changing careers because they have realized that the field of medicine or law is no longer for them and there are workers changing careers because they're ready to strike out on their own and start a business. Which reader is your ideal reader?

You have to choose. A book that has the potential of appealing to everyone ends up appealing to no one. The more specific you can be, the more impact your book can have.

Once you know why your ideal reader is coming to your book—their deep need—you can extrapolate to the wider target audience for the book and identify secondary audiences. You'll learn about that step when you work on the book proposal in Part 4.

....

Who is Your Ideal Reader?

In her book, *The Widest Net,* small business influencer Pamela Slim recommends defining your ideal customer first by their challenge or aspiration rather than by demographics. "You have to have a clearer way to understand which problems they are trying to solve," she writes, "otherwise, you will waste huge amounts of time and resources spreading your message to a broad and generic audience."

Readers come to nonfiction books for very specific reasons—for education, entertainment, insight, information, or for belonging and cultural currency. They *want* something. You can look at your own book-buying habits to see precisely how this works.

Here, for example, are some of my recent book purchases and the reasons I made them:

- I've recently read a lot of books on the history and current state of race in America (*So You Want to Talk About Race* by Ijeoma Oluo, *The Anti-Racist Writing Workshop* by Felicia Rose Chavez, *Kindred* by Octavia Butler) because I was made aware by recent events that there was a lot I didn't know and a lot I needed to learn. Many of my friends, family, and colleagues were reading these books as well, and I wanted to be part of the conversation. I sought these books out with a great deal of intention to expand my perspective. My need was education and cultural currency.

- I bought a book called *Burnout* by Emily Nagoski and Amelia Nagoski because I heard a Brené Brown podcast with the authors and thought they would have something to teach me about resilience and handling powerful emotions, which are often a trigger for migraines. I did not seek this book out the way I did the books on race, but once I heard about it, it touched on a topic that is of great interest to me—I have had migraines for 30 years. I bought it because I thought it might increase my self-awareness and my overall wellness. My need was better health.

- I bought Pam Slim's book, *The Widest Net,* which I quoted earlier, because I have been coached by Pam in the past and know her to be a brilliant and insightful guide to running a small business. I thought it would help me do a better job of coaching my book coaches. My need was to improve my business skills.

So, what is your ideal reader looking for? What problem are they trying to solve? Think of the point your book is making and then consider your reader's desire or pain around that point. Why do they need what you're offering?

It can help when you're doing this exercise to think of someone you know. It could be a client or a colleague, a mentee or your 20-year-old self. Why are they buying a book? What are they looking for?

CASE STUDY #1

Who is Your Ideal Reader? by Dr. Jennifer Noble

How old are they, and where do they live?

My ideal reader is 35-55 (old enough to have a teen, possibly kid is old enough to be headed to college). She lives in a big, well-furnished/designed home with her partner and a big backyard for her kids. They have an expensive breed of dog. She lives in a "nice" neighborhood—Culver City, Playa Vista, Beverly Hills, Santa Monica, Palos Verdes, Brentwood, Pacific Palisades, Calabasas, etc. She is an educated parent of teens who works a lot and makes a good salary. She is a mom who maybe voted for Bernie, loves Elizabeth Warren and is inspired by AOC. She definitely loves Obama (especially Michelle) and was excited about the possibility of Hillary Clinton.

She sends her kid to Campbell Hall school in Studio City or Crossroads in Santa Monica (almost 40k/yr). She is a mother who is focused on achievement and who believes achievement is an indicator of the type of person you are. She is a mother who will take her child to Subway for a quick dinner and remind their child that they better do well on their homework lest they "end up working in Subway." She buys her kids designer clothes and enjoys the compliments of others on how her children look or are dressed. She plans elaborate birthday parties with very specific themes that are considered "original" (pasta making at the local cooking school with a chef or paint and sip at the local art school with a painting instructor). She may not always cook dinner as she works quite a bit. The family may not eat dinner together often due to the busy schedules of the children. Her children may have their own rooms, with their own

TVs for their own video games and their own smartphones and laptops.

What keeps them up at night?

This mom stays up worrying about her kids' future. She worries if her child is good enough, whether their grades are good enough, if they are playing the right sports or interested in the right careers. She worries if they are taking the right classes and working hard enough in them. She worries they spend too much time with their friends. She worries all the work and money she is spending is in vain because her teen may not be taking their future seriously enough. She worries whether her child will get into a "good university" and good usually indicates a top ranked school that neighbors would find impressive. This mother worries that one mistake she or her child makes can ruin his future and he will not be able to earn a high income or have a well-respected career.

What do they want more than anything in the world?

This mother wants her child to be successful and important, and by this she means have money. She wants her child to have wealth, possibly because her own family did not have as much or perhaps because her family did and taught her to believe it as a way to be important. Money to this mom means her child is worthy. If her child were to choose to not go to college and run a churro stand by the beach at the Santa Monica Pier (or work in Subway), this would devastate her.

She wants her teen to feel important in the world, to feel worthy and of value. She does not see that the importance and worth her child will feel would come from society and not within. Having or earning money and status is the way she teaches this character trait of self-worth.

What can your book do to help them get it?

My book will help this mother see that by focusing on money as a way to achieve self-worth, she is actually missing key aspects of parenting, as well as teaching a fear and devaluation of those with less money. She is actually teaching classism (and by default racism). She is teaching a sense of entitlement and a belief that others with less money are not good people, are unworthy and don't deserve to be treated as equals or deserve access to the things money can afford. She is also instilling a sense of anxiety that will not easily be reduced because the child will not have a clear sense of how much money will finally equal their self-worth.

CASE STUDY #2
Who is Your Ideal Reader? by Michael Melcher

How old are they, and where do they live?

26-35. Washington, D.C., originally from barrio of South Dallas.

What keeps them up at night?

On the outside, Gabriel seems easygoing, pleasant to be with, someone who can mix with the bro's without doing offensive things. He takes care of his clothes (bought at Nordstrom Rack) and wears preppie shoes (leather shoes without visible socks). He works hard at his job as a junior associate at a law firm but doesn't come off as a grind or hyper-achiever.

That said, he is deeply ambitious. He has depended on himself ever since childhood. He usually doesn't speak first in a group because he's learned to read the environment well. He knows code-switching backwards and forwards. He is more political than people think.

He is more radical than his employees realize (they've never asked him about DACA) yet is also very interested in being successful in mainstream employment, including the private sector. He once took a Chicano studies seminar and while he found the ideas interesting, he couldn't imagine living in cruddy graduate housing for the next ten years teaching bored sophomores about identity and power structures.

So, overall, easygoing on the outside but intense on the inside. Friendly. More alone than people realize but not lonely.

What keeps them up at night?

Imposter complex—this shows up in the fear that he will have made one small mistake (mis-citing a holding or making a verbal faux pas) that will cause everything to collapse. He wonders if he is right to buckle down for a few years in this job or if he should make a more dramatic step and move back to Texas to start running for political office.

Sometimes he wonders whether he will really achieve his political ambitions or just be a competent but unimpressive lawyer who maybe gets on the school board in a boring suburb after 20 years, as opposed to being Senator. He wonders how meaningful personal relationships fit into this career equation.

What do they want more than anything in the world?

He wants to be an elected politician. He wants to be elected a U.S. Senator. He wants to be big, accomplish things that help his own community and others. He wants to live out the American dream, big time. He wants his parents to be proud and be able to have a comfortable retirement. He wants to inspire all the other Gabriel Beltrans who didn't quite make it to where he has.

What can your book do to help them get it?

This book will give Gabriel a roadmap to make the career decisions he needs to and have comfort that he is doing the right steps—so he can just do them and not worry about them. It will be the roadmap that works for him—a highly ambitious and hardworking brown person who has made it far but wants to make it farther. It won't seem to be written for a privileged white person nor will it seem to be written for one of his cousins working at AutoZone who don't have the ambitions or opportunities.

TAKE ACTION

- If you thought of a particular person for your ideal reader, write down their name.

- Write half a page about who this person is in terms of demographics:

  » How old are they?

  » Where do they live?

  » What is their income level?

- » What is their education level?
- » Do they have a specific race or ethnic origin or gender?
- Write half a page about the problem your book will help this person solve.
  - » What keeps them up at night?
  - » What do they want more than anything in the world?
  - » What can your book do to help them get it?

....

What Transformation Are You Promising?

In fiction, we describe the reader transformation journey by looking at the protagonist's arc of change. The reader steps into the protagonist's shoes to experience the world from their point of view as they struggle to achieve something they desire. The opening and closing scenes are bookends that contain the story, and the path from one to the other is the transformation journey. We want to see the character confront their desires and the obstacles in their way and become someone new. We want to see *movement*. A book that does not have this kind of movement feels flat and ineffectual.

The same thing must happen with a nonfiction book, but in nonfiction, it's the *reader* who undergoes a change. They start out in one place: a place of being unaware or unsure or uninformed or uninspired. And they end up in another place: a place of knowing something new, understanding something new, embracing something new, believing something new.

Defining the transformation you promise is a key step in making sure you deliver it. Just as you did with your own motivation in *Blueprint Step #1*, it helps to think about external and internal goals. What will your reader get externally from your book? Will she lose weight, make money, have a better relationship with her mother, be able to start an organic farm? What will she get internally? Will she feel more confident, more knowledgeable, ready to take a new kind of action?

To define the transformation journey, we need to ask two questions:

What is the Start of the Journey?

The first step is to figure out where exactly the book will begin. This goes back to your ideal reader and the problem they are seeking to solve (*Blueprint Step #6*), and to the point you are making in the book (*Blueprint Step #3*). What does your ideal reader want or need? Where exactly are they in the process of acquiring the knowledge you're going to give them?

Are you, for example, teaching someone the basics of how to plant a simple vegetable garden or are you teaching an advanced course on growing enough food to feed a family? Are you teaching someone how to get over their fear of public speaking or are you teaching someone how to deliver a talk on the main TED stage? If you are trying to teach college graduates about personal finance, are you going to assume they have no savings, no family support, and a ton of student debt? Or are you going to assume that they are pocketing their entire paycheck and living in an apartment their parents happen to own? If you are trying to teach your reader about how to get better sleep and your solution has to do with meditation, are you assuming they have never tried meditation or have they tried but they don't believe it will work for them?

In my introduction to this book, I said I assume my reader wants to aim for excellence; I am not speaking to people who want to write quickly or who don't have the desire to think deeply. I am also assuming that my reader wants to *write* their own book—to raise their voice and claim the power of becoming a thought leader; they are not in search of a ghost-writer. They want to write, but they are overwhelmed about all the decisions they have to make and a bit embarrassed about how much they don't know about book publishing since they know so much about their area of expertise. These are their pain points and the decisions I made about the beginning of my readers' arc of change.

What Is the End of the Journey?

Where will your ideal reader be at the end of your book? How will they have changed? In addition to the external knowledge they might gain (how to save 10 percent of their income, how to sleep through the night, how to be anti-racist, how to write a nonfiction book), think about the internal change. Will they have faith, confidence, self-awareness, a sense of peace, a sense of belonging?

CASE STUDY #1
The transformation journey of a book about writing a nonfiction book by Jennie Nash (this book!)

My goal is for my reader to gain knowledge about how to write a book. My point is that the way to reduce overwhelm and write something powerful is to think before you write—to plan, to be strategic, to be intentional. But what I ultimately want is for my reader to feel confident that they can actually do it, so that instead of talking about writing a book, they will indeed actually do it. So, the transformation journey for my ideal reader looks like this:

- At the beginning, my ideal reader wants to write a book, but they aren't sure how to proceed. They are nervous about what they don't know. They don't have time to waste and want guidance they can trust.

- At the end of the book, my reader can visualize their book inside and out. They know who it's for and how it fits into the marketplace. They feel confident in the proposal they have developed, and in their ability to write the book. They are ready to pitch.

CASE STUDY #2
The transformation journey of a book about the healing impact of houseplants by Karen Hugg

- At the beginning, my ideal reader is busy and stressed out, inside all the time, tweaking with constant random thoughts, and yearning for peace. They lie in bed at night wondering if they can make ends meet before getting sucked into the whirlwind of the day, navigating commitments in a mostly indoor world of work, school, and home where screens, not nature, dominate their lives. They appreciate nature and how important protecting our environment is, and so are already pre-disposed to explore its happy-making effects. But oftentimes they don't know how.

- At the end of the book, readers discover how to consciously use nature's healing effects to reduce stress and increase happiness within whatever space they have. They have learned how to disengage from screens and find more time in their busy lives. They know how to destress through plants and create their own plant-oriented space to indulge in Green Leisure at home and maintain the habit.

TAKE ACTION

- Describe the problem or challenge your ideal reader has when they come to your book.
- What will they know or feel or believe when they are finished? What will they be ready to do?

What Other Books Speak to Your Ideal Reader?

In this step, the goal is to make a list of five books similar to yours that your ideal reader has already turned to for help.

The purpose of compiling a list of comparable titles, which you'll include in your book proposal, is to give agents and editors a context for your book and to help you understand the marketplace you are entering. You'll sometimes hear people use the word "competitive" to describe this list of books, but you're not in competition with other books; you're in community with them.

I like to think of comp titles like this:

The books that are already sitting on the shelf are having a conversation. You want your book to be part of the conversation. Why do these books speak to your ideal reader? What will your book add to the conversation? Pretend that the books are having an actual discussion. One is saying one thing and the other is saying, "Yes, and..." or "No, but...." They are agreeing, arguing, debating, joining together in a chorus. You know what the point of your books is, so where in the conversation does your book fit?

If you were writing a book about nutrition during pregnancy, your book would probably be read after *What to Expect When You're Expecting*, because you know that almost every pregnant woman gets that book the second she finds out she's pregnant. You would be adding more depth and nuance to an idea that *What to Expect* spends just a few pages on. That is one conversation. Another conversation might be the one your book has with a general book on nutrition for women or with a popular diet book that everyone is reading that you believe could be risky for a pregnant woman.

If you were writing about business leadership, what would your book say about Brené Brown's *Dare to Lead*? Would it say, "No one in the bond trading business actually talks about being vulnerable—that's ridiculous. We think of daring in a totally different way. Let me explain." Or would it say, "Brené has such great ideas—so how do you actually implement them if you run a business in the world of higher education? I will show you how." Or would it say, "Vulnerability is only half the story. The other half is _____."

The biggest mistake a writer can make is to say, "There has never been another book like mine!" Most readers buy multiple books on the same topic. When I was planning a trip to Korea, for example, I bought four. When I was diagnosed with breast cancer, I bought dozens. I probably own several hundred books about writing.

People in publishing don't want to hear that there has never been another book like yours (and they probably wouldn't believe you anyway.) They look to existing books to gauge how yours might do and to get a sense of the market. They want your book to share attributes with other books that have done well. Doing some research can help you frame your book in a way that will give agents and editors clarity and confidence.

Which Books to Choose

- Select books that have been published in the last two years.

- Stay with nonfiction titles unless there is a memoir or a novel that is perfectly aligned with your book. If, for example, you are writing a book about how to raise a tennis champion, you might want to include Andre Agassi's memoir, *Open.* If you are writing a cookbook that riffs on Julia Child's work, you might want to consider including *Julie and Julia*, a memoir about one woman who set out to cook every single one of Child's recipes.

- For writers seeking traditional book deals, avoid including self-published books unless you know they have sold exceptionally well.

Where to Dig for Comparable Titles

Start the comparable titles search by looking for books to compare to yours. Here's how:

1. What are the best-selling books in your category? This is a great place to start. It can be very tricky to get sales data for *any* book, so you will probably be looking at bestseller lists on Amazon and big review outlets like *USA Today* or the *Wall Street Journal* to get this information. Don't fall into the trap of listing *only* bestsellers. You want to think about the whole

universe of books that resonate with your readers, not just the ones with the biggest name recognition.

2. When you find a book that is a candidate for a comparable title, check out the Amazon feature entitled "Customers Who Bought This Item Also Bought…" (That feature is listed below the description of the book. Scroll down until you see recommended books lined up across your screen.) Add any potential comparable titles to your list.

3. Consider books outside of your category that speak directly to your ideal reader. This can be a smart way of framing your book. Let's say, for example, that you have written a book about how to launch a start-up. Including a memoir by a famous start-up founder might be a great way to frame the universe your book will exist in, because all your target readers will have read the memoir and have it on their shelf. Michael Bungay Stanier says he often compares his business management book *The Coaching Habit* to artist Austin Kleon's *Steal Like an Artist.* On the surface, a book about coaching in the workplace might not have anything to do with a book about making art, but Stanier drew a line between the structure and accessibility of Kleon's book and his own, and it makes perfect sense.

4. Dig into the books on your list. If you haven't read them all, that's OK. Go look them up on Amazon, Goodreads, or on the shelves of your local bookstore. Read the book jackets and the reader reviews—the good, the bad, and the ugly. Get a sense of how people talk about the books, what they feel about them, and what each means to them.

PRO TIP: *While searching for comp titles, you might come across a book that is very much like the one you want to write—and this can sometimes send you into a tailspin. You may think your project has been grounded before it even took off. But don't despair. You may think that someone has already written the book you want to write, but that's not possible. No one can write your book because no one is you. No one's brain is looking at things the same way or drawing on the same experiences that you are. Figure out what you are saying that they are not, what you are offering that they are not, and how you can serve your reader in a way that they are not.*

CASE STUDY #1

Comp title brainstorm for *Braided: A Journey of Thousand Challahs* by Beth Ricanati, MD.

Beth made a list of books from the three categories that define her book: self-help/wellness, cookbooks, and memoirs. This was a long list that needed to be trimmed down, but starting this way helped her understand that her book was bridging three distinct categories. Here is her list:

Challah Cookbooks

- *The Secret of Challah* by Shira Wiener and Ayelet Yifrach

- *A Taste of Challah* by Tamar Ansh

Food Memoir

- *The (Faux) Pastry Chef: How I Found My Baking Fix* by Mimi Shotland Fix

- *Eating the Bible: Over 50 Delicious Recipes to Feed Your Body and Nourish Your Soul* by Rena Rossner

- *Bread & Wine: A Love Letter to Life Around the Table with Recipes* by Shauna Niequist

- *The Kitchen Counter Cooking School: How a Few Simple Lessons Transformed Nine Culinary Novices into Fearless Home Cooks* by Kathleen Flinn

- *Julie and Julia: My Year of Cooking Dangerously* by Julia Powell

- *A Homemade Life: Stories and Recipes from My Kitchen Table* by Molly Wizenberg

- *Egg: A Culinary Exploration of the World's Most Versatile Ingredient* by Michael Ruhlman

Self-Help/Wellness

- *The Blessing of a Skinned Knee: Raising Self-Reliant Children* by Wendy Mogel, Ph.D.

- *The Modern Jewish Mom's Guide to Shabbat: Connect and Celebrate—Bring Your Family Together with the Friday Night Meal* by Meredith L. Jacobs

CASE STUDY #2
Comp title brainstorm for *Happy Campers: 9 Summer Camp Secrets for Raising Kids Who Become Thriving Adults* by Audrey Monke

Camp director Audrey Monke found a wide range of comparable parenting books that she thought her ideal reader would know and love. Here is her list:

- *The Blessing of a Skinned Knee: Raising Self-Reliant Children* by Wendy Mogel, Ph.D.

- *The Price of Privilege: How Parental Pressure and Material Advantage Are Creating a Generation of Disconnected and Unhappy Kids* by Madeline Levine, Ph.D.

- *How Children Succeed: Grit, Curiosity, and the Hidden Power of Character* by Paul Tough

- *The Whole-Brain Child: 12 Revolutionary Strategies to Nurture Your Child's Developing Mind* by Daniel J. Siegel and Tina Payne Bryson

- *The Gift of Failure: How the Best Parents Learn to Let Go So Their Children Can Succeed* by Jessica Lahey

- *How to Raise an Adult: Break Free of the Overparenting Trap and Prepare Your Kid for Success* by Julie Lythcott-Haims

TAKE ACTION

- Make a list of 10 comparable titles for your book.
- If you learn anything that helps you clarify your idea, take good notes. This is a great time to go back and hone your point and refine your ideal reader's pain.
- Pare your list down to the five titles that best put your book in context.

How Will You Connect with Your Ideal Reader?

Now that you know something about your ideal reader, you can think back to the why that you defined in *Blueprint Step #1* and think more specifically about how you will connect with your readers when your book is in the world.

For this step you want to consider your zone of genius in terms of promotion and marketing. If you hate social media, it makes no sense to build a marketing plan rooted in social media. If you are terrified of public speaking, you don't want to rely on reaching readers from a big stage. You want to connect with readers where you can shine.

One of the best ways to think about connecting with your ideal reader is to see how other authors you admire are doing it. Go to the webpage of a writer whose book you love and look for an Events or Appearances page. Visit their social media channels. Study what they are doing—how are they engaging with readers, what resonates with you? What you would love to be doing when it's your turn?

- Will you be teaching workshops? If so, where? A middle school? A community center? A corporate boardroom?

- Will you be interacting with your audience on social media, doing chats and giveaways and live events?

- Will you be attending book clubs? Speaking on podcasts? Writing op-eds?

- Will you be forming strategic partnerships with other people or organizations in your field to reach a shared audience?

- Will you be testifying on Capitol Hill? Giving a TED Talk? Headlining a conference?

- Will you develop an ecosystem of products and services that build on your book?

PRO TIP: *If you get stuck, it helps to get very granular. What does a great day look like when you are an author with your book in the world? What are you eating—lunch on the go? A fancy meal with investors? What are you wearing—jeans and a travel-friendly sweater? A fabulous jacket? What are you doing? If your answer to all these questions is, "I don't want to do any marketing of any kind, I just want to write," you probably need to re-think your stance. In today's publishing universe, authors are expected to connect with readers.*

CASE STUDY #1
How Will You Connect with Your Ideal Reader?
by Michael Melcher

Michael Melcher, the executive coach who we heard from in *Blueprint Step #2,* has an extensive professional network. He knew he would connect with his ideal reader through that network. He is also a podcaster and a very experienced conference presenter. When asked how he imagined connecting with his ideal reader, Michael wrote a very short and sweet answer:

> I picture myself giving a talk on a big stage. I do a great job and afterwards, people come up to speak with me and invite me to speak to *their* audiences, but one young brown woman hangs back waiting for the crowd to part. She nervously approaches me. "Your book changed my life," she says, "It cracked the code for me. I wanted to thank you."

I love this story because it is so specific. Michael fully pictured himself as an author in the world. He saw himself commanding a stage at an event and connecting with a certain kind of person in a profound way. He was seeing himself changing lives.

CASE STUDY #2
How Will You Connect with Your Ideal Reader?
by Susanne Dunlap

Susanne is a very accomplished piano player. Her book is about women composers from the Middle Ages to the present. She imagines connecting with her ideal reader through music:

I am not my target reader, but I have good ideas about how to reach her. Because the primary audience is children/ young women, I would probably mainly reach her through parents and music teachers. Because of the age, groups on social media wouldn't be the right way to go about getting the book into her hands, although an Instagram campaign with quotes and pictures might work.

I would do outreach to schools with music programs and bands/orchestras. Giving a presentation is ideal, because playing the music composed by these women adds an enriching dimension to the book.

In addition, I have musicology contacts all over the world from my days as an academic, and I would reach out to mine them for introductions to any people they know in the middle-school/high school music world.

Locally, I was the managing director of Pioneer Valley Symphony for five years and I know many music teachers in schools throughout Western Massachusetts and Vermont. As Director of Development for Connecticut Opera years ago, I also still have contacts in Northern Connecticut.

TAKE ACTION

- Write a few paragraphs about how you will connect with readers in the real world.

PART 3

. . . . . .

Design a Structure

One of the most common questions I get from writers is some form of this: "Is my idea any good?" Sometimes it is posed slightly differently (e.g., "Do you think this book has a chance of landing an agent?" "Can you tell me if this is worth pursuing?" "Do you think people will care?" "Am I likely to make any money?")

The best answer is a quote by Lemony Snicket, the protagonist of the children's book series, *A Series of Unfortunate Events* by Daniel Handler, who said, "It is never the story and always the way it is told."

In other words, ideas are cheap. It's how you handle your idea, how you present it, how you pin it to the page that matters. At a certain point, "the way a story is told" is about the content you are presenting and the language and voice you use to present it, but before you get there—long before you get there—the way it is told refers to structure.

How, in other words, is your idea contained and constrained? What limits have you put around it? Where are the edges of the idea? These are questions about structure.

Choose a Structural Prototype

The structure of a book refers to the overall shape or form of the idea—how it is organized, how it functions. It is bigger than the outline of the book or a list of its contents (which we will get to in a moment). The structure you select has a profound impact on how your reader will experience the material and what they will take away from it.

Think of a book like *Eat, Pray, Love*—a book that is (in a very blunt analysis) about saving yourself by getting out of your comfort zone—and how that story would have been different if it had been any other number of idea/place combinations besides three. If it had been just one place, it could have been a story about a person's relationship to a place like *A Year in Provence* by Peter Mayle. If it had been a whole lot of places, it could have been something like Anthony Bourdain's *A Cook's Tour: Global Adventures in Extreme Cuisines*. If it had been 1000 places, it could have become an aspirational how-to travel book like *1,000 Places to See Before You Die* by Patricia Schultz.

Changing structure can sometimes entirely change the kind of book you are going to write, your ideal reader, your point, and everything else about the project—which is fine.

It's more than fine. The *Blueprint* process is all about finding clarity and defining your book idea.

Stealing Structure

The wonderful thing about structure is that you can adopt someone's structure. Or as Chip and Dan Heath put it in *Made to Stick: Why Some Ideas Survive and Others Die*, "Don't think outside the box. Go box shopping. Keep trying on one after another until you find the one that catalyzes your thinking. A good box is like a lane marker on the highway. It's a constraint that liberates."

I am not advocating literal stealing. You can't write about the work of becoming an artist in a 12-step process like Julie Cameron did for *The Artist's Way* and call what she calls "morning pages" something like "a.m. pages"—that would just be wrong and weird and possibly illegal, unless you were building on her work in a very specific way she had blessed, or perhaps satirizing it and acknowledging your debt to her idea.

But you *can* do something like this:

For years, I was struggling with a book I wanted to write about migraine. I was struggling with my point, my ideal reader, and my structure. I was lost, but the idea of writing about migraine wouldn't let me go. One day, I was doing some research for a client, and I read an excerpt from Glennon Doyle's *Untamed*. She has an unusual structure for her story about coming into her whole true self—three conceptual/ideological sections (cages, keys, free), that tell a tale with entries in those sections that are presented in a non-chronological way. This structure was like a lightning strike to my idea about migraines. I could immediately see how what I was trying to do would come alive with a fractured structure like that. I could suddenly *see* the book I wanted to write, and so I adopted that structure for my own material and my own purposes.

That's what you are looking for—the structure that brings the idea to life.

The Three Nonfiction Prototypes

Let's look at the three basic structures for nonfiction books. There are, of course, far more than just three, but we'll focus on these to simplify things. As I describe each one, try to imagine your material taking the shape I am describing. Is it a natural fit? Or is it like putting a square peg into a round hole? If the latter, that's a red flag. You need to make sure your structure serves your material.

This way of looking at your book is taking a mile-high view. It's not the table of contents—that comes next. If you were building a house, you would be deciding what kind of house—sprawling ranch house for a big family or small bungalow for a newlywed couple—not laying out the rooms and certainly not picking out tile and paint color.

1. Single Narrative

This way of writing a book tells one story, from beginning to end, in a roughly chronological narrative format. I say roughly, because chronologies can be fractured, or presented out of order, but those are stylistic choices. The basic structure of the book is still a single narrative. These kinds of stories can either be memoir (the author's own story), reported stories about another individual, or reported stories about a situation, entity, event, or group of people.

The "single" in the title of this structural prototype refers to the fact that the narrative is focused on one single story. *The Premonition* by Michael Lewis, for example, chronicles a group of scientists and public health professionals who were working on a plan for controlling a pandemic before the pandemic; their stories are woven together and make up the threads of the single narrative about the U.S. public health system and contagion.

Examples of memoir include:

- *Eat, Pray, Love* by Elizabeth Gilbert – a memoir of one woman's journey around the world to find herself.

- *Maybe You Should Talk to Someone* by Lori Gottlieb – a memoir of a therapist who goes into therapy.

- *A Three Dog Life* by Abigail Thomas – a fractured narrative about a woman whose husband suffers from a brain injury.

Examples of reported stories about an individual include:

- *The Immortal Life of Henrietta Lacks* by Rebecca Skloot – a journalist investigates what happened to the cells of Henrietta Lacks when they were used for research.

- *Midnight in the Garden of Good and Evil* by John Berendt – a reporter covers a murder trial in Savannah, Georgia.

Examples of reported stories about a situation, entity, event, or group of people include:

- *Into Thin Air* by Jon Krakauer – the story of an ill-fated Mt. Everest expedition.

- *The Premonition* by Michael Lewis – an exploration of the individuals who knew the pandemic was coming and tried to stop it.

- *She Said* by Jodi Kantor and Megan Twohey – a behind-the-scenes story of the two *New York Times* journalists who broke the Harvey Weinstein scandal.

2. Collective Narrative

This way of writing a book presents a collection of narratives about one topic. The author does not make an effort to weave the stories into one cohesive whole the way they might when writing a single narrative; they are curating different voices or different interviews and putting them in a specific order. One of the included stories may be the author's own story.

Examples include:

- *Tribe of Mentors: Short Life Advice from the Best in the World* by Timothy Ferriss – a compilation of advice from 130 of the world's top performers.

- *Moms Don't Have Time To: A Quarantine Anthology* by Zibby Owens – essays from a variety of parents and writers about surviving the pandemic.

- *Cherished* by Barbara Abercrombie – stories about cherished pets from a variety of writers, including the author.

3. Conceptual Design

In these kinds of books, the concept or topic you are writing about drives the organization. You are teaching your readers something through a proven framework, and you are likely including primary research, observations, or experiences to support your point. The structure is designed to explain that framework or concept. Examples include:

- *Bird by Bird* by Anne Lamott – Lamott shares stories about the writing life and also teaches distinct lessons along the way. The stories are selected and placed to illustrate the lessons. Much of this book feels like memoir because Lamott shares stories from her life, but the intent of the book is very explicit: to teach the reader how to live the writing life. It is, therefore, shelved in the bookstore in the writing reference, not the memoir section.

- *The 4-Hour Workweek* by Timothy Ferriss – A book about how to work less and earn more.

- *Made to Stick* by Chip Heath and Dan Heath – A book about how to craft a message to help your business attract sales and buzz.

- *Freakonomics* by Steven D. Levitt and Stephen J. Dubner – an economist presents a rogue theory about economic incentive.

- *Quiet* by Susan Cain – a book about being an introvert in a noisy world.

- *The Life-Changing Magic of Tidying Up* by Marie Kondo – a theory for cleaning house based on the concept of joy.

- *Colleges That Change Lives* by Loren Pope – a list of 40 colleges that will change the way you think of college.

- *1,000 Places to See Before You Die* by Patricia Schultz – a collection of awe-inspiring travel spots.

- *The Barefoot Contessa Cookbook* by Ina Garten – A collection of delicious recipes.

- *Don't Sweat the Small Stuff* by Richard Carlson – A collection of tips, insights, and inspiration for stress-free living.

The structure you choose can dramatically change what your book will become. If you are unsure about the best way to proceed, play around with the structures. At this moment in the creative process, I always think about wet clay. Your material exists and has some kind of form and weight, but it could still be a bowl, a pitcher, or a vase.

Take my book about migraine. I knew I wanted to write about migraine but was not sure what kind of book I wanted to write. If I were to write a memoir, it would be the story of a woman's effort to come to terms with pain and uncertainty. If I were to chronicle other people's experiences with migraine along with mine, it would be a collective narrative—a kind of *Chicken Soup of the Soul*. If I were to write a guided journal about how to track your migraine triggers, that would be a conceptual structure—even if I included entries about my own experience with triggers in every chapter. If I were to tell the stories of the various professionals fighting for migraine to be taken seriously as a disease (a fantasy I had back in the day when there were no effective medications), that might be a single narrative.

If you find that none of these structural protypes works for the book you want to write, and you are certain the foundation of your idea is strong—meaning the rest of your

Blueprint answers hang together and describe a cohesive whole—it may be that you will need to combine these structures into a unique hybrid model, or come up with something new and unusual to fit the book you are envisioning.

TAKE ACTION

- Which structure do you think you'd like to adopt? Just write it down, and in the next step we'll dig deeper to see how, exactly, the structure will serve your story.

Breaking Down Each Structure

For each structural prototype, I developed a series of cornerstone questions to help you make sure that the structure you chose is a good fit and to help you understand the purpose and power of your book even more.

I pose the questions and then answer them for an existing book so you can get a sense of how they work to flesh out your structure. These answers are my interpretations, not the authors' ideas.

Single Narrative: Cornerstone Questions

1. **What is the main spine of the story?** What's the central plot the reader will follow? What is the main action the reader will follow?

2. **What hurdles stand in the way of the protagonist(s) as they try to achieve their goal?** Answer on two levels: the external level (what happens in the world) and the internal level (what holds the protagonist back? Their ego? Their doubt? Their belief that the world is a dark and evil place?)

3. **What period of time does the book cover?** It's critical to know the timeframe you are writing about. The story may start earlier, which you can address in a flashback or through dialogue, but knowing the boundaries of your "canvas" is critical. Answer with a period of time, such as "two weeks," "the 2004 NBA season," or "14 years."

4. **Where will the book start – specifically?** I want you to name the exact scene you envision as Scene 1.

5. **Where will it end – specifically?** Stories usually end when the struggle that began in Scene 1 is resolved.

6. **Where is the narrator standing in time as they narrate the story?** Has the story already happened and you are looking back on it? In this case, you would have the benefit of wisdom gained from the experience. If the story is unfolding while you tell it, you must preserve the innocence of not knowing.

CASE STUDY #1: SINGLE NARRATIVE
Creativity Inc by Ed Catmull and Amy Wallace

Q: What is the main spine of the story?

A: The main plot of *Creativity, Inc* is the story of how Pixar Animation figured out how to bake creativity into the fabric of their business and along the way created a company that nurtures and celebrates the creative process.

Q: What hurdles stand in the way of the protagonist as they try to achieve this goal?

A: On the outside, the company had to figure out how to be both profitable and creative. They faced challenges related to technology, financing, competitors, and personnel. On the inside, they faced challenges related to their own high standards and to the need to say yes and no to the right projects.

Q: What period of time does the story cover?

A: The story spans from Catmull's 1960s graduate-school dream of making a computer-animated movie called *Pi* to the release of *Toy Story* in 1995 to Steve Jobs' death in 2011. (Jobs purchased Pixar in 1986.)

Q: Where will the story start—specifically?

A: The book begins with a story from the height of Pixar's success but quickly moves to talking about Catmull's love for *The Wonderful World of Walt Disney* TV show as a kid and how his dream of making a computer animated movie was nurtured.

Q: Where will it end—specifically?

A: The story ends with a company-wide memorial for Steve Jobs in 2011.

Q: Where is the narrator standing in time as they narrate the story?

A: Catmull is narrating his story from the present day. He has the wisdom of knowing how it all turned out and is sharing the lessons he learned along the way.

TAKE ACTION

- If you are writing a Single Narrative, answer these corner-stone questions:

  1. What is the main spine of your story? What's the big idea?

  2. What hurdles stand in the way as you try to achieve this goal or as you struggle toward what you are after?

  3. What period of time will your story cover?

  4. Where will the story start—specifically?

  5. Where will it end—specifically?

  6. Where are you standing in time when you narrate it?

Collective Narrative: Cornerstone Questions

  1. **What is the main point of your story?** What's the big idea? This is a chance to refine what you wrote about your point earlier in the *Blueprint*.

  2. **What is each of the entries going to be about, on a very big-picture level?** What, in other words, connects them?

  3. **How will the pieces be arranged?** Will they start and end in such a way that there will be an overall transformation journey for the reader? Is there some other way you will present the material?

  4. **What are the *limits* of the scope of this big idea?** Are there obvious things about the topic you will NOT cover in the book? Will you ask the participants not to write about certain elements?

5. **How many pieces will you include?** A book with 12 entries is going to be very different from a book with 200. Know your scope.

6. **How will your own voice play into the story?** Will you be writing the introduction and nothing else? Will you write intros to each piece? Will one of your pieces be included in the mix?

CASE STUDY #2: COLLECTIVE NARRATIVE
My Ideal Bookshelf by Jane Mount

Q: What is the main point of your story?

A: *My Ideal Bookshelf* celebrates the pivotal place books play in our lives by presenting books as highly intimate, physical touchstones, and by offering a challenge readers can take to create their own ideal bookshelf.

Q: What is each of the entries going to be about on a very big-picture level?

A: In each entry, a leading cultural figure speaks briefly about the 10 books that would sit on their ideal bookshelf. Each entry is illustrated with the spines of their chosen books.

Q: How will the pieces be arranged?

A: They are arranged alphabetically, which dictates each entry's placement. There is space at the end for the reader to make their own ideal list and illustrate it.

Q: What are the limits of the scope of this big idea?

A: There are physical limits. Each essay about the books must fit on one page. Each illustration must fit on the facing page. There are, however, no conceptual limits to what "ideal" means. Each cultural figure gets to choose what "ideal" means to them—books that have been the most cherished, the most impactful, books they would take with them to a desert island, books they keep near them, etc.

Q: How many pieces will you include?
A: 100.

Q: How will your voice play into the story?
A: The only visible appearance of the author's story is in the introduction to the book. Most of her work is behind-the-scenes, curating the list and editing the interviews of contributors. All the illustrations in the book are by the author.

TAKE ACTION

- If you are writing a Collective Narrative, answer these cornerstone questions:

  1. What is the main idea of your story? What's the big idea?

  2. What are each of the entries going to be about on a very big-picture level? What, in other words, connects them?

  3. How will the pieces be arranged?

  4. What are the limits of the scope of this big idea? Are there things you will NOT cover in the book?

  5. How many pieces will you include?

  6. How will your voice play into the story?

Conceptual Designs: Cornerstone Questions

1. **What is the organizing concept or principle?** Why does the book exist—to teach something, lead us to an understanding, offer a new perspective? This touches on the transformation journey and the point of the book.

2. **What does your table of contents look like?** What is the scope of the content and how does it flow? (Note that there is more information on how to develop the TOC in *Blueprint Step #12*. Here, just give a quick sketch.)

3. **Is there a specific order to the way you present the material, or some other kind of logic to the way the material flows?** Are there timelines or steps? Describe the flow of material.

4. **What are the elements of each chapter?** Are there quotes? Interviews with experts? To-do lists? Checklists? Places to write answers to questions? Create a chapter template so you can see exactly what it will look like.

5. **Is your own story part of the mix?** How much of your own story? How much of the mix?

CASE STUDY #3: CONCEPTUAL DESIGN
Real Happiness: The Power of Meditation by Sharon Salzberg

Q: What is the organizing concept or principle?
A: The book walks readers through a 28-day program to achieve happiness through meditation.

Q: **Is there a specific order to the way you present the material, or some other kind of logic to the way the material flows?**

A: The meditation challenges get progressively harder each week, and the solutions that are presented get progressively more difficult. So, you start out just sitting a few minutes and breathing, and you work up to meditating for much longer periods of time.

Q: **What does your table of contents look like?**

A: There are two introductory chapters about meditation—what it is and why it works. Then the book starts a Week 1, Week 2 structure—through Week 4. This is the meat of the book, where exercises are given and questions answered. The final chapter is "The Weeks Beyond" about how to sustain the practice. Each week tackles a different part of the meditation challenge: concentration, mindfulness and the body, mindfulness and emotion, and loving kindness.

Q: **What are the elements of each chapter?**

A: Each chapter includes an introduction, a "Practice Review" (an overview of what will be taught), meditations to try (there is a CD included with guided meditations), reflections, and "the Takeaway."

Q: **Is your own story part of the mix?**

A: The author of this book is a meditation teacher. She shares her own experiences and the experiences of various students and mentors.

PRO TIP: *Some books have repeatable structures in each chapter—meaning that every chapter contains the same basic elements. If yours will, you will need to sketch out a chapter template. Once you do this, you essentially have an outline for the whole book and can "fill in the blanks" when you begin writing. Elements of a repeatable structure might include: quotes, stories (those of the author or other people), case studies, expert interviews, sections with subheads, sidebars, lists, quizzes, questions, charts and graphs, key takeaways, and action items.*

TAKE ACTION

- If you are writing a book with a Conceptual Design, answer these cornerstone questions:

  1. What is the organizing principle?

  2. Is there a specific order to the way you present the material, or some kind of logic to the way the materials flows? Are there timelines or steps? Describe the flow of material.

  3. What does your table of contents look like?

  4. What are the elements of each chapter?

  5. Is your own story part of the mix? How much of your own story? How much of the mix?

....
Design a Table of Contents

The previous step had us looking at structure in terms of the overall organization and design of the book. In this step, we will zoom in and focus on your book's content through the development of a table of contents.

The TOC is much more than a simple outline of what material will be included in the book. It's where your idea comes into focus, your structure gets solidified, and you can begin to really think big. Think of the table of contents as the secret to ensuring that your book delivers the transformation your reader is looking for. A great TOC shows the reader how your book will propel them toward their specific and desired goal. Books like Michael Pollan's *Cooked* and *The Top Five Regrets of the Dying* by Bronnie Ware do this. I love that kind of power and clarity because it can only come from someone with deep experience who has wrestled an idea onto the page and who is determined to serve their reader.

The idea of wrestling is important here. You're trying to pin your idea down. To do that, you need to ask yourself, what belongs in the book and what doesn't? You may need to make some hard choices, but the good news is that your idea is still malleable. You haven't written any pages yet. You can try out a dozen different TOCs. You can go back and choose a different structural prototype, or redefine your ideal reader, or select a new title.

Gretchen Rubin, author of 10 books, including the mega bestselling books, *The Happiness Project* and *The Four Tendencies,* told me that it took her more than a year to land on the TOC for her tenth book, an exploration of the five senses which she describes as "how I'm getting back inside my body by collecting color, eating ketchup, and making daily visits to the Met."

Gretchen started this book as she always does, with a question: how can I live more fully in my body? On her blog, she wrote, "For too long, I've treated my body like the car my head is driving around town, and my prediction was that by getting back inside my body by systematically exploring my senses, I could shake my mind awake." She knew she would be researching the subject and exploring the senses in her own life, and she knew that the book would present a combination of her findings and her experiences, but for more than a year, she was not sure about the shape of her TOC.

At one point, she was struggling with a TOC that had more than 28 different senses. Here is how she described that process to me, and how it resolved:

"We all know the basic five senses—see, hear, smell, taste, touch. You could call those the kindergarten senses or the Aristotelian senses. But if you do the research, you find out that scientists talk about 28 senses, maybe as many as 33 senses. I was not interested in talking about things like proprioception, or interoception, but at the same time, I did feel like there were these more basic senses that preoccupied us all the time—things like pattern, our sense of other people, and our sense of time.

I did all this research, and I'm investigating all this, and wondering how do I organize everything? And I mean, the sweat is just pouring down my face. I'm trying to figure out how everything fits together. Is nine the right number of senses? I'm adding, subtracting, combining. And then one day, I was describing it to my daughter, and she said, 'I kind of think you should just talk about the five senses.'

And I thought, *Oh my gosh, you're right. I should just talk about the five!* In that moment, the book became much more coherent and clear. The structure became obvious."

As you design your idea, the best resources you have are the ones you have already developed in this *Blueprint*. Look again at your ideal reader and what they need. Look at your point and the transformation journey you are promising them. Study the answers you gave to the question of structure. Ask yourself:

- Do all of the pieces hold together?

- Do they feel as though they are part of a coherent whole?

- Can I envision this book and how it will help my reader?

- Can I create a TOC that feels elegant, obvious, and resonant—one I can't wait to flesh out?

If you can't, don't despair. This is the step where things often really come together for a book—and where things are most likely to fall apart. But you have the tools you need to shore everything up if you find flaws or weaknesses in your idea. You just work through the *Blueprint* until everything clicks.

Just like Gretchen described, you'll know it when you have it right. You'll feel it in your gut, and the great news is that your reader will also feel it when they pick up your book one day. They'll know in an *instant* what the book is and that it is right for them.

Let's look at two great TOCs for inspiration:

CASE STUDY #1
The Five Love Languages by Dr. Gary Chapman

I bring up *The Five Love Languages*—a relationship self-help book—to all kinds of writers all the time, including those writing business books, parenting books, and wellness books, because it perfectly illustrates what a great structure can do for a topic. I find it useful because educators, entrepreneurs, and executives will often laugh at me when I mention it: They immediately dismiss it as off-topic and sometimes as frivolous. But this allows me the chance to say, "But wait! Look at how from the title alone you immediately know what this book is and who it's for and who it's not for. There's something powerful in that, right?" When they reluctantly agree, we go look at the TOC and see that the title is only the start of this book's power.

At this point, I usually point out that I have never actually read *The Five Love Languages*, nor do I own it. Everything I know about this book, I learned from the TOC, from

the author's website, and from excerpts I read on Amazon—
which is an incredible testimonial for it. The book broadcasts
its point and its message loud and clear. The form serves its
function. This is why it's such a good example to use for writers trying to find their point and their message.

Take a look at the TOC for *The Five Love Languages*:

1. What Happens to Love After the Wedding?
2. Keeping the Love Tank Full
3. Falling in Love
4. Love Language #1: Words of Affection
5. Love Language #2: Quality Time
6. Love Language #3: Receiving Gifts
7. Love Language #4: Acts of Service
8. Love Language #5: Physical Touch
9. Discovering Your Primary Love Language
10. Love is a Choice
11. Love Makes the Difference
12. Lovely the Unlovely
13. A Personal Word

- Notice how concise it is. It takes just a few lines to
  show the transformation journey the reader is going
  to take

- Notice how the very first chapter centers on the reader
  and the problem—you know exactly who this book is
  for (married people) and exactly what the problem is
  that the book is trying to solve (a disconnect in how
  love is expressed).

- Chapters 2 and 3 address how to solve the problem.

- In Chapters 4 through 8, we get into the specifics of the method the author is presenting. I do not even have to read these pages to understand what this method is and how it works—and there is no way to read this TOC and not start thinking about where you yourself fit in this universe. It draws you in, engages you, gets you thinking, gets you curious.

- Chapter 9 is the heart of the book—and every time I look at this TOC, I am curious about which mine is (it's a toss-up between Acts of Service and Words of Affirmation—or maybe Physical Touch!). I wonder what the author will do to guide me to select the primary one, and even as a reader of just the TOC, I am happy that he is going to lead me through that dilemma. I know I am in the hands of an authority—someone who knows this material cold and has clearly walked many people through it.

- The rest of the book is about how to use this information to improve upon your relationship—to choose love. This is the big takeaway. You have the power to know how you tend to express love, to know how you like to receive it, to know what your partner's tendencies are, and to choose love. Who wouldn't want this?

I use this table of contents as an example because I want you to develop a TOC that is this clear, this solid, and this well-designed for your ideal reader and their core problem. I want you to design something that has the ability to be this viral. I don't just want you to write about whatever topic you are writing about in a way that is logical (although that's a solid start). I want you to write about it in a way that broadcasts your message like a lighthouse beaming across a foggy sea.

CASE STUDY #2
The Artist's Way by Julie Cameron

Some of the most beloved nonfiction books adapt a structure from an unusual source—another industry or another way of thinking. *The Artist's Way*, for example, famously uses the 12 steps of addiction recovery to address the problem of being creatively stuck. Even if you have never been to an Alcoholics Anonymous meeting, you instantly understand the framework and the point: that you have to be as intentional about recovering your creative equilibrium as you would be about getting sober.

Borrowing the structure gives the new idea an additional layer of power. Julia Cameron could have easily written her book about getting unstuck by listing out all the things that keep you stuck and talking about ways around those blocks. That would have been a good book. But would it have been a mega-seller? Without the 12-step association, without the 12-week plan, without the idea of recovery underpinning it? My guess is not. Here is a truncated view of the TOC:

Introduction

Spiritual Electricity: The Basic Principles

The Basic Tools

Week 1: Recovering a Sense of Safety

Week 2: Recovering a Sense of Identity

- Notice (again) how concise this TOC is. One glance and you get it: This is a 12-week recovery program.

- Notice the impact of the repetition of the word "recovering". It makes you realize that this is a practice to engage in, one that never ends, and one that you can be improving on all the time. The form helps us get the message immediately. It also lets us know that the author is going to bring compassion and understanding to the teachings.

- In the complete TOC (not pictured here), exercises and check-ins in each chapter let the reader know that this is a workbook. They will need to be actively engaged if they want to get unstuck.

- At the end is a Creativity Contract. You know where you are heading with this book and what will be asked of you, and commitment is part of it.

- The TOC shows that the author is taking the reader on a journey of transformation. We can see it, we can feel it, and odds are good that if we need it, we are going to buy this book before we even read a single page. The TOC sells it.

Chapter Length and Book Length

As you plan out your TOC, you will be thinking about dividing the material in terms of chapters. A chapter covers one specific idea and connects to the other chapters that come before and after it—a connection we will discuss in more depth in the Outcome Outline in *Blueprint Step #13*.

Chapters give a book its order. They provide natural breaks where the reader can breathe and reflect.

How long should each chapter be? That depends.

One thing to know is that publishers think in terms of word count, not in terms of pages. A standard typewritten page on a computer—with 12-point Times New Roman font and 1-inch margins all around—is about 250 words. Two hundred of those pages is 50,000 words. A typical range for a nonfiction book is 50,000 to 80,000 words. Your word count might be shorter if you are writing a highly illustrated book or a so-called "gift book," but it probably won't be much longer.

Overall word count informs the design of your chapters. A book that only has six chapters is going to have much longer chapters that one that has 26. If you have a lot of chapters or very distinct sections to what you are teaching, you might also consider dividing the chapters into sections or parts.

Debbie Millman's book *Why Design Matters: Conversations with the World's Most Creative People* is organized into five sections called Legends, Truth Tellers, Culture Makers, Trendsetters, and Visionaries. She described to *Fast Company* magazine her experience designing the TOC. Referencing her wife, author Roxane Gay, Millman said:

> "Confession: Roxane helped me with that. I felt that there needed to be a way to organize them (the chapters) that also gave you permission to stop reading or start in a different place."

TAKE ACTION

1. Write out a simple Table of Contents. Use no more than one page.

2. Name your chapters.

3. Write one sentence to describe the contents and the point of that chapter.

....
Create an Outcome Outline

Having a strong structure and a good Table of Contents is only the start of writing a great book. The contents of your book also need to flow from beginning to end and draw the reader in. This is a concept known as narrative drive. It's the thing that keeps the reader engaged enough to keep turning pages. If there is no narrative drive, your book runs the risk of just being a bunch of interesting ideas jammed together—and that is a recipe for losing your reader.

To build narrative drive, you name the point or outcome of each chapter and the outcome you intend the reader to experience, and then you state how that outcome *directly leads into the next chapter's point*. The Outcome Outline tracks and tests the interior logic of your book. Think of it like a breakdown of the overall transformation journey.

There are three columns in an Outcome Outline:

- **Column 1: Point.** This describes the point of the chapter. You can use the one sentence you wrote in the TOC exercise, or revise it to be even more specific.

- **Column 2: Outcome.** What is the outcome of this chapter? What will your reader know or feel or be doing by the end of the chapter? Think both externally and internally like you did when working on the transformation journey as a whole.

Note that sometimes the outcome of a chapter might be similar to the ones around it. If a reader is building their confidence as they read forward in your book, the outcome could be "the reader feels a sense of increased confidence" in several chapters. In this case, you need to make sure that the chapters are different enough to warrant taking up precious real estate in your book. Are they making different enough points about confidence? Are they moving the reader forward in their transformation?

- **Column 3: "Because of that."** This is where you link one chapter to the next. "Because of that" is language taken from fiction. We use it to describe a cause-and-effect trajectory of a character's actions: "Because the protagonist did X, Y happens." For nonfiction, the progression is: "Because the reader now knows X, they can now learn about Y." Locking chapters together in this way guarantees that each chapter drives to the next one, and that together they drive toward the overall point of the book.

The Seven Point Outcome Outline Checklist

Once you have filled in the columns, use this checklist to test whether your outline is doing everything it needs to do:

☐ Check that at the beginning of the Outcome Outline, your reader's problem or challenge is clearly stated. Is the problem they would come to this book to solve obvious?

☐ Check that each chapter has a distinct point that is related to the overall problem or challenge the reader is reading the book to solve. If the point of the chapter is extraneous, consider deleting that material.

☐ Check that each chapter has a distinct point that is different from all other chapters. If not, delete a chapter or combine chapters that are making the same point.

☐ Check that each chapter delivers a specific outcome. Is it clear that the reader will end up with new information or a new understanding at the end of it?

☐ Check that the outcome of each chapter leads logically and directly to the outcome of the next chapter.

☐ Check that the reader ends up in a different place at the end of the book from where they began. Has a transformation happened? Is the outcome of the last chapter directly related to the problem or challenge stated in Chapter 1?

☐ Check that there is one clear point to the whole book. What does your reader know, believe, or understand that they didn't before?

CASE STUDY #1
The Outcome Outline for *Compose Yourself: The Essential History of Musical Women Who Broke the Silence and Dazzled Their World* by Susanne Dunlap

Susanne's book is a Conceptual structure. It's a book about female composers. She knew she wanted to tell the stories of these women in a roughly chronological order. She decided to feature 12 composers. This is her simple table of contents, developed in the last step:

Introduction, or when it comes to women in history, silence isn't golden
A brief introduction to why women composers aren't household names today.

Chapter 1: Hildegarde the hermit (don't try this at home) (early 11th–12th century)
This medieval mystic lived in a monastery from somewhere between the age of 8 and 14 for decades before founding her own order and writing haunting music at the time when music notation was new.

Chapter 2: Beatriz, Countess of Dia and the romance of the troubadours (12th–13th centuries)
One of the few trobairitz (women troubadours) whose music has been preserved from a unique time in the Midi—which is now southern France—when an entire culture of toleration and openness existed.

Chapter 3: Francesca Caccini: from Starling to Composer in the Medici court
First woman ever to compose an opera, commissioned by another woman: Maria de Medici—who became queen of France.

Chapter 4: Elizabeth Claude Jacquet de la Guerre at the court of Versailles
The only woman composer to be famous in the sun king's court, taken under the wing of Athenais, Madame de Montespan, notorious mistress of Louis XIV.

Chapter 5: Anna Magdelena Bach, or the curse of a famous husband

She was an accomplished musician and probably composer but busy bearing Bach thirteen of his 23 children.

Chapter 6: Marianne Mozart, Sister Act

She might have been a better violinist than her brother—but girls weren't supposed to play the violin. And as a composer—did she pen some of Mozart's early work?

Chapter 7: Maria Theresia von Paradis, blind to the prejudice against her

Being a woman wasn't her only disability when it came to making a career as a musician and composer, but she made a name for herself in Vienna.

Chapter 8: Fanny Mendelssohn Hensel—another talented sister

Granddaughter of a famous philosopher, sister of a famous composer, but they wouldn't let her publish her music or even perform in public. Ironically, it was her husband who encouraged her to defy her family and publish.

Chapter 9: Clara Schumann and her mad husband, or women can do everything, right?

Child prodigy pianist who married a famous composer. They had lots of kids, and he ended up on a madhouse—but she had to keep going.

Chapter 10: Alma Mahler, the bad girl who made good music

She was a bit of a tearaway, but she didn't let the social strictures of the time stop her.

Chapter 11: Amy Beach, Boston's first woman symphonic composer

Almost through the 19th century, audiences looked to Europe for classical symphonic music. Bostonian Amy Beach went a long way toward changing all that.

Chapter 12: Nadia Boulanger, the woman who taught great men composers more than a thing or two

Leonard Bernstein, Aaron Copland, Astor Piazzola—Just a few of the most famous composers of the 20th century who studied with this French woman

Conclusion: You really can do anything you want in music these days

Opportunities for women have opened up since the mid-20th century.

When you read Susanne's short TOC, you might think that her book is no more than a collection of short biographies of interesting women composers. You might wonder what the point of the book is, or what the transformation journey for the reader is. In other words, the content in the TOC might strike you are being a bit flat and ineffectual.

This is where so many writers go wrong. They put their contents in a logical order and call it day. But there is so much more work that can be done to make the contents come to life.

When Susanne developed her Outcome Outline (below), she proved that there is nothing at all flat and ineffectual about her book. You can see that there is a purpose to each chapter being here and that they each add up to a moving whole. You can see, in other words, that in organizing her book in this way Susanne is telling a powerful story and making a profound point for her ideal reader.

	POINT	OUTCOME	BECAUSE OF THAT . . .
CH.	*Why is this chapter here? What is the experience of the reader in this chapter?*	*What will reader know or feel or be doing by the end of the chapter? Where are they on the journey?*	*How is this chapter connected to the next one? What is the idea that moves the reader from this chapter to the next?*
1	This chapter introduces the reader to the fact that there's a whole history of western music she might not be aware of.	I imagine my reader will be curious, and perhaps a little surprised, and want to discover more	The general concept moves to specific historical examples, proof of what I talk about in this first chapter
2	Western music history basically begins in the middle ages because there was no music notation before then. Hildegard of Bingen (1098-1179) was a mystic who wrote treatises and liturgical music at a time when women were barely educated and the church was a patriarchal hierarchy. Her most famous work was the Ordo Virtutem.	I think the reader will be amazed that a woman could have done so much at a time in history that was so unfamiliar, that she was unafraid of the powers that be and used every weapon at her disposal to make them bend to her will and acknowledge her power.	Her influence was pervasive, but no woman really followed her. The next chapter moves from liturgical music to secular (which I will define).
3	When societies are open and tolerant, remarkable artistic products can flower, and women are capable of participating fully. However, at this time, women with enough education and leisure were from the upper classes, as is our example, Beatriz, Countess of Dia (1175-1212).	This exploration of a vanished culture that produced a unique musical environment is also an indictment of the damage that the restrictive patriarchy can have on the lives of women, not just politically, but artistically. I think a reader might feel a little sad about this.	Once this culture vanished after the Albigensian Crusades, women composers sort of vanish from history too. The plague and wars had something to do with it all, of course, but it isn't until the Italian Renaissance/early Baroque that we find another documented woman composer.

	POINT	OUTCOME	BECAUSE OF THAT . . .
CH.	*Why is this chapter here? What is the experience of the reader in this chapter?*	*What will reader know or feel or be doing by the end of the chapter? Where are they on the journey?*	*How is this chapter connected to the next one? What is the idea that moves the reader from this chapter to the next?*
4	We know more about composers in the Italian Renaissance as music notation became printable, not just needing to be copied by hand. This is also the beginning of musical dynasties, and a flowering of secular music—which made it possible for women to enter the picture again (since they couldn't work within the Church's musical hierarchy). It not only helped, it was probably a requirement to have a musical parent or two if a girl wanted to be a composer—which is the case with Francesca Caccini.	Francesca Caccini (1587-1641), daughter of Giulio, went from being an extraordinary singer (dubbed The Starling by Cosimo de Medici) to being a composer. Marie de Medici, who became the wife of Henri IV of France, and then the famous regent of Louis XIII, commissioned Francesca to write an opera (a very new genre) on the subject of Alcina and Ruggiero, from Ariosto's epic poem. Not much of her music survives, which is often the case with music of that period. But women had a modicum of power and autonomy at that time. And this, I hope, would give the reader cause for a bit of hope.	The Baroque period continued to see a flowering of secular music, again providing opportunities for women composers and performers. Where vocal music was predominant in the Renaissance, purely instrumental music began to surface as the baroque period changed light-hearted dance music into something more serious. Perhaps this was because of Louis XIV's penchant for ballet.

		POINT	OUTCOME	BECAUSE OF THAT . . .
CH.		*Why is this chapter here? What is the experience of the reader in this chapter?*	*What will reader know or feel or be doing by the end of the chapter? Where are they on the journey?*	*How is this chapter connected to the next one? What is the idea that moves the reader from this chapter to the next?*
5		Elizabeth-Claude Jacquet de la Guerre (1665-1729) earned a position in Louis XIV's court not just as a performer, but also as a composer. She, like other women we've seen so far, had a musical family and powerful allies.	Jacquet de la Guerre was, like Caccini, first a performer, only her instrument was the harpsichord. She became part of the court of Louis XIV when she was a teenager, and was under the supervision of the king's notorious mistress, Madame de Montespan. She married a musician and even then composed and performed throughout Paris. Again, her limited success might be cause for a false sense that things are on a steady upward climb for women composers.	At this time, people (men) were starting to write about music, leaving records of what they thought of different composers and works. Elizabeth was so highly regarded, that a man who wrote a treatise about the best musicians of the day included her in the list— but as a performer rather than as a composer.

	POINT	OUTCOME	BECAUSE OF THAT . . .
CH.	*Why is this chapter here? What is the experience of the reader in this chapter?*	*What will reader know or feel or be doing by the end of the chapter? Where are they on the journey?*	*How is this chapter connected to the next one? What is the idea that moves the reader from this chapter to the next?*
6	During the High Baroque period—and all the time before there were recordings or other live entertainment (no movies, no tv etc.)—composers were often attached either to a church or a court and under pressure to produce new music all the time. That was Bach, who in addition to composing a vast catalogue of work, also had 23 children from two wives. His second wife, Anna Magdalena (1701-1760), was a singer in the court he worked in. But recently, scholars have questioned whether some of Bach's works were in fact composed by her. She was a busy lady, who also bore 13 of Bach's children.	Being part of a musical family can be a double-edged sword if you're a woman. It can be difficult to make your voice heard over that of your male relatives, and the burdens of childbirth and other expectations can interfere with any thought of a musical career as well. The musical institutions started to become even more male-centered at this time, possibly indicating a narrowing rather than a widening of possibilities. Also, getting music performed was an expensive and politically motivated enterprise. The men held the purse strings, so if a woman wrote an ambitious orchestral or choral work, say, getting it performed would be very, very difficult. This was the beginning of limiting women to writing chamber music, that could be performed in the home by a few musicians. I'm afraid the reader might start getting a little depressed at this point.	This is the beginning of the true, male-dominated musical canon: Bach, Mozart, Beethoven. These figures cast a huge shadow over the 18th and 19th centuries, and being a woman composer at that time was, if anything, more fraught with disappointments and difficulties than it had been before.

	POINT	OUTCOME	BECAUSE OF THAT . . .
CH.	*Why is this chapter here? What is the experience of the reader in this chapter?*	*What will reader know or feel or be doing by the end of the chapter? Where are they on the journey?*	*How is this chapter connected to the next one? What is the idea that moves the reader from this chapter to the next?*
7	Musical prodigies were all the rage in 18th-century Europe. Everyone knows the story of Mozart playing the keyboard for the Emperor of Austria when he was three. But he had an older sister, Maria Anna (called Nannerl, 1751-1829)) who was probably just as talented. In fact, Mozart looked up to his older sister, and they went on tour together as children. She played the harpsichord and the violin, but was discouraged from the violin because it wasn't a suitable instrument for a lady. Interesting that Nannerl coincided with the blind Austrian composer, Maria Theresia von Paradis, who knew Mozart and for whom he probably wrote a piano concerto. She deserves her own chapter.	There are no extant compositions by Nannerl, but surviving letters from Mozart to his sister praise her compositions, so it's clear she was writing them. It seems that her father was very domineering, even ending her career as a performer as soon as she was of marriageable age. It's hard to know what she might have done if she could have had free rein. This will definitely piss off the reader.	Rather than moving women in music forward and progressing toward more equal representation and opportunities, the late eighteenth, early nineteenth centuries saw even more limitations. [Perhaps a mention of the Napoleonic code.] This was partly due to the romantics in literature, who made the image of the suffering (male) artist popular. Women weren't capable of producing great art or literature because they lacked something, apparently. The irony is that we know more about women composers in this period, simply because there are more surviving records.

	POINT	OUTCOME	BECAUSE OF THAT . . .
CH.	*Why is this chapter here? What is the experience of the reader in this chapter?*	*What will reader know or feel or be doing by the end of the chapter? Where are they on the journey?*	*How is this chapter connected to the next one? What is the idea that moves the reader from this chapter to the next?*
8	Maria Theresia von Paradis (1759-1824) lost her eyesight sometime between the ages of 2 and 5. She wasn't from a musical family, but her father was wealthy and well-connected, a minister in empress Maria Theresa's court. She had enough means to commission works from other composers, and she was well known as a performer around Vienna and on tour. It was on tour that she apparently started composing pieces for herself to perform. Later, she turned to grander works, eventually composing five operas and three cantatas. Irony: it was the failure of her opera about Ruggiero and Alcina (remember Caccini above?) that turned her more toward teaching than composition.	Paradis's blindness added insult to injury when it came to trying to carve out a career as a musician and composer. But her experience in that world led her to establish a music school for young girls in Vienna in 1808. She taught them piano, singing, and music theory, and featured their compositions in public concerts. Here, a woman is taking steps to widen opportunities for other musical girls, which might give the reader cause for hope that things do eventually open up.	The relatively little known Paradis leads to the more famous Fanny Mendelssohn Hensel, sister of Felix. This could also lead to a discussion of the way opportunities were closed to Jews at the time, that the Mendelssohn children had to convert to Catholicism in order to be accepted in society and eligible for certain opportunities. It wasn't just women who had trouble getting ahead.

	POINT	OUTCOME	BECAUSE OF THAT . . .
CH.	*Why is this chapter here? What is the experience of the reader in this chapter?*	*What will reader know or feel or be doing by the end of the chapter? Where are they on the journey?*	*How is this chapter connected to the next one? What is the idea that moves the reader from this chapter to the next?*
9	Fanny Mendelssohn Hensel (1805-1847) was the older sister of the more famous Felix Mendelssohn. They were devoted to each other. Fanny was a superb pianist and composer, but her father would not permit her to perform in public or publish any of her work. She had a private recital hall (the family was wealthy) and invited guests could come to hear her. In fact, her early works were published under her brother's name. It wasn't until she married that any compositions were published under her own name, and her family disowned her for it.	Here's irony about Fanny: as one of her brother's friends wrote, "Had Madame Hensel been a poor man's daughter, she must have become known to the world by the side of Madame Schumann and Madame Pleyel as a female pianist of the highest class." In other words, rather than opening up opportunities, being of a wealthy class actually made it more difficult for her to have a career, because it wasn't seemly for her to perform in public. So gender and class are both factors. I hope by this point, the reader is really getting the picture of how it was for women in music in previous centuries.	Fanny's compositions were virtually unknown until the 1990s, when scholars dug them up. That's when interest in many of these forgotten women blossomed. But Clara Schumann (as the quote in the previous section might indicate) was already known to many because of the circumstances of her life.

	POINT	OUTCOME	BECAUSE OF THAT . . .
CH.	*Why is this chapter here? What is the experience of the reader in this chapter?*	*What will reader know or feel or be doing by the end of the chapter? Where are they on the journey?*	*How is this chapter connected to the next one? What is the idea that moves the reader from this chapter to the next?*
10	Clara Wieck Schumann (1819-1896) was a child prodigy. She made her official concert debut at the age of 9. Her music-teacher father, Friedrich Wieck, pushed her hard to try to make his fortune as a teacher by taking her on tour everywhere, and using her to lure students to him. One of those students was Robert Schumann. Clara and Robert fell in love, but he was much older than Clara, and her father did not approve. They had to go to court to get permission to marry. Wieck's objections weren't just due to Robert's age; he also probably deduced that the composer was mentally ill. Robert was confined to a mental asylum for the last 2 years of his life, leaving Clara to provide for their 8 children.	Clara must have been super human. She performed, taught, composed, and raised a family all at the same time, with a husband who was brilliant and famous, but very unstable. But Robert was unusual in recognizing his wife's talent in composition: "Clara has composed a series of small pieces, which show a musical and tender ingenuity such as she has never attained before. But to have children, and a husband who is always living in the realm of imagination, does not go together with composing. She cannot work at it regularly, and I am often disturbed to think how many profound ideas are lost because she cannot work them out." She became the only female teacher on the faculty of a music conservatory. She mostly taught women, but a few men, and 68 of her students went on to have their own musical careers.	By now all the obstacles stacked up against women composers throughout history must be obvious to the reader. We're also coming to the end of the 19th century, and still women don't have access to jobs conducting orchestras or teaching composition in music schools and conservatories. This was as slow to change as attitudes were.

	POINT	OUTCOME	BECAUSE OF THAT . . .
CH.	*Why is this chapter here? What is the experience of the reader in this chapter?*	*What will reader know or feel or be doing by the end of the chapter? Where are they on the journey?*	*How is this chapter connected to the next one? What is the idea that moves the reader from this chapter to the next?*
11	Mrs. H.H.A. Beach (Amy Beach 1867-1944) is the first American composer we've covered. She was also the first successful American woman composer of large-scale symphonic works (as opposed to just chamber music, or concertos for her own performance). Her Gaelic Symphony was premiered by the Boston Symphony Orchestra in 1896. She was pretty extraordinary: among other things, she taught herself to read at age 3.	However, when she married Mr. Beach (24 years older than she was), he made her agree never to teach piano, to limit her own performances to two a year with profits donated to charity like a good society matron, and—ironically—to concentrate on composition instead— but she wasn't allowed to study with anyone. After he died, she resumed her performing career and also taught. She had had to put her career on hold because of society's expectations. The point being that even with decades in between, determined women have been able to take their place in the musical world	Amy Beach is a step closer to women having respected careers in music, but there was still a long way to go, and the idea of being "ladylike" and well-behaved still got in the way of a woman making a musical career.

	POINT	OUTCOME	BECAUSE OF THAT . . .
CH.	*Why is this chapter here? What is the experience of the reader in this chapter?*	*What will reader know or feel or be doing by the end of the chapter? Where are they on the journey?*	*How is this chapter connected to the next one? What is the idea that moves the reader from this chapter to the next?*
12	The beginning of the 20th century was the beginning of women's awakenings, demands for more rights etc. (including suffrage). Alma Mahler (1879-1964) was a famous beauty, a fact that worked both for and against her. She was a very talented pianist and composer, but her affairs and wild life have been written about more than her music. Her first marriage was to Mahler, who didn't want her to compose once they were married. She became a devoted wife and champion of her husband's music. Only when he found out she was having an affair with an architect did Mahler take any interest in Alma's compositions. He had his own publisher bring out five of her compositions a year before he died (1911).	Sometimes people decide to interpret strength and talent in women as bad behavior. But Alma faced life on her own terms, never giving up music and love.	Change is in the air for women in music. They still weren't allowed in most institutions that resulted in musical jobs, but they were making inroads. The next woman wasn't just a composer. She became a renowned teacher of composition through the 20th century.

	POINT	OUTCOME	BECAUSE OF THAT . . .
CH.	*Why is this chapter here? What is the experience of the reader in this chapter?*	*What will reader know or feel or be doing by the end of the chapter? Where are they on the journey?*	*How is this chapter connected to the next one? What is the idea that moves the reader from this chapter to the next?*
13	Nadia Boulanger (1887-1979) came from a musical family, and believed she had no talent for composition herself. Nonetheless, she was smart and knew enough to teach it to many famous composers throughout the 20th century. She also became a conductor of orchestras—another occupation forbidden to women. When she was very young, she hated music and used to hide when it was being played. This all changed when her mother got pregnant with her sister when Nadia was 5, and she suddenly became so interested in music that she studied to enter the conservatory. Her father was 72 when her sister was born, and she may have felt she had to find a way to support the family.	It's odd that Nadia didn't think she had a talent for composing, as she won prizes for it when she was a student at the conservatory, studying with Gabriel Fauré. She wrote many successful compositions and came close to winning the Prix de Rome, but she was convinced her compositions were worthless. Nadia never married, and so never had to negotiate for the right to lead her musical life the way she wanted to. [She may have been gay, although I'd need to do more research about this. She had a student who stayed with her for 14 years, then became a teacher and close friend and companion for the rest of her life.] The point? Even through the 20th century, with many more opportunities opening up for women in music, it helped that Nadia didn't have to answer to a husband and fulfill his expectations.	We're getting close to the present day, when many, many more women are composers and conductors, but even today, there is no parity.

	POINT	OUTCOME	BECAUSE OF THAT . . .
CH.	*Why is this chapter here? What is the experience of the reader in this chapter?*	*What will reader know or feel or be doing by the end of the chapter? Where are they on the journey?*	*How is this chapter connected to the next one? What is the idea that moves the reader from this chapter to the next?*
14	Conclusion: It can seem like a miracle that we have any record at all of women composers from as long ago as the middle ages. As years went on, more and more of them (list some that weren't covered).	It's easy to think these days that women can achieve just as much as men in any field—which they mostly can. But the ground was prepared by women in previous centuries who held fiercely to their talent and ambition to do what they were told they shouldn't do.	Go make music!

CASE STUDY #2
The Outcome Outline for *Share Like It Matters* by Dan Blank

Here is an example of an Outcome Outline by my friend Dan Blank, a book marketing expert. His working title is *Share Like It Matters* and the book is about the importance of sharing what you make and connecting with an audience in an authentic way. It's a how-to book (Conceptual Design), with a table of contents that follows a framework for developing skills around marketing and sharing creative work.

This Outcome Outline is a work in progress (with a confusing mix of first, second, and third-person points of view) but you can still feel the way the book draws the reader in and pulls us through. You can still tell that, even though the book is primarily designed to educate, Dan is also telling a story. His authority over this material is crystal clear.

	POINT	OUTCOME	BECAUSE OF THAT . . .
CH.	*Why is this chapter here? What is the experience of the reader in this chapter?*	*What will reader know or feel or be doing by the end of the chapter? Where are they on the journey?*	*How is this chapter connected to the next one? What is the idea that moves the reader from this chapter to the next?*
1	**Give Yourself Permission** People wait for permission from others to really dive into creating and sharing. This chapter talks about turning up your own volume and giving a greenlight to your creative vision, from the act of creating, to ensuring it reaches someone in a meaningful way. The biggest barrier to your creative dreams is yourself. Don't create halfway and share without passion. We explore the most pervasive narratives people tell themselves that stop them from creating and sharing, including that it is too late, that they missed their chance, that they are behind everyone else. In this chapter, you will become a student of how people create and share, in order to understand it as a natural part of your own life.	You have an inner sense of permission to create and share.	Once you have permission, you need to move past the inner boundaries that hold you back.

	POINT	OUTCOME	BECAUSE OF THAT . . .
CH.	*Why is this chapter here? What is the experience of the reader in this chapter?*	*What will reader know or feel or be doing by the end of the chapter? Where are they on the journey?*	*How is this chapter connected to the next one? What is the idea that moves the reader from this chapter to the next?*
2	**Embrace Your Boundaries** Here I talk about how the boundaries that you feel hold you back are an essential part of the creative process. All great art had hard boundaries. I explain the concept of Creativity Cave Trolls, help the reader identify their own, and find ways to manage them. We also explore how to move through social risk and identify models for success to turn boundaries into gateways.	You will identify the inner narratives and beliefs you have which hold you back from creating and sharing. And you will learn how to move through them.	One you reframe your boundaries, you need clarity of what you create and why. Otherwise, you will be unable to clearly communicate and share your work.
3	**Get Radical Clarity** Here we go deep into understanding not only what you create and why, but also how this is the foundation for what you can share with others. Through exercises, you will get clarity on what your message is and why it matters to others. This is a critical step to knowing how to effectively share your work in a way that will truly resonate with people. This chapter also covers how to present yourself to the world, and describe what you create.	You will have a clear sense of what you create and how to communicate that to others.	Once you have clarity on what to create and how to communicate it, you need to better understand the person you hope to reach. Too many creators get lost in vague inspiration and endless research. By understanding who you hope to reach, we demystify a faceless audience into real people you can connect with.

	POINT	OUTCOME	BECAUSE OF THAT . . .
CH.	*Why is this chapter here? What is the experience of the reader in this chapter?*	*What will reader know or feel or be doing by the end of the chapter? Where are they on the journey?*	*How is this chapter connected to the next one? What is the idea that moves the reader from this chapter to the next?*
4	**Know the Person You Hope to Reach** It's impossible to share your work when you have to think of them as a massive faceless audience. Flip how you think of what it means to have an audience for your work by thinking about individuals that you hope to reach. Then, get to know them. That will demystify so much of what you need to know about how to share your work effectively.	You will know who you hope to reach with your creative work, where to find them, and what engages them.	Now that you know what to share and who you want to reach, you need a system so that you don't wake up each day panicked at what to share.
5	**Create a Sharing System** I introduce a series of tools that helps create a system around what you can share and when. It is part of a strategy that solves for the issue that so many writers and artists face: they feel they have no time and no energy to share their work. Many people resist the idea of a system because it feels inflexible and like yet another thing they have to live up to. But the system is meant to work for you, not you for the system. When you consider the radical clarity you defined for your creative work, this system is meant to help you live up to it.	You will understand what you can share that feels authentic to who you are, and engaging to your ideal audience, and develop a system to make it easy.	Once you have a sense of what to share and how, we have to be sure that you don't become a "content machine" just measuring which content "worked" and which "didn't." If you want engagement, you have to engage through meaningful experiences. We need to directly address the connection between creative work and your identity.

	POINT	OUTCOME	BECAUSE OF THAT . . .
CH.	*Why is this chapter here? What is the experience of the reader in this chapter?*	*What will reader know or feel or be doing by the end of the chapter? Where are they on the journey?*	*How is this chapter connected to the next one? What is the idea that moves the reader from this chapter to the next?*
6	**Your Identity is an Experience** This chapter challenges people to view their creative vision not as a product in the marketplace, but an experience that it creates. This is the bridge to explaining how the creative work itself connects to the idea of the creator having a platform. It also takes a more realistic view of what success looks like. It isn't the sale of a book, it is having someone READ the book and being moved by it. I challenge the reader to double-down on their creative vision and make it a core part of their identity.	You will forge your identity through meaningful moments with your ideal audience.	Most creators share then retreat. They do the minimum amount possible to share what they create and their process of doing so. Instead, they need to approach this with vigor, with enthusiasm, and with a wonderful empathy that is required to connect it with others.
7	**Connect with Others with Authenticity and Generosity** Too often, writers and artists focus on the content and channels, but ignore the best way to truly engage others: through authenticity and generosity. Here we focus on practical ways to engage others, expand your network and infuse it all with a sense of generosity and deep fulfillment.	You will know how to develop your network and community with a sense of authenticity.	Organic marketing and outreach offer a strong foundation, but how will you reach new people? The next step is to consider how a marketing campaign can spread your message and help you find new people who will love your work.

	POINT	OUTCOME	BECAUSE OF THAT . . .
CH.	*Why is this chapter here? What is the experience of the reader in this chapter?*	*What will reader know or feel or be doing by the end of the chapter? Where are they on the journey?*	*How is this chapter connected to the next one? What is the idea that moves the reader from this chapter to the next?*
8	**Focus People's Attention** If you truly want someone to support your work, you have to create reasons for them to engage and ways that it brings them together with others. In this chapter we dig into how to create effective marketing campaigns that get people talking.	You will understand how to create marketing campaigns that not only spread the word about what you create, but feel fun to be a part of.	Know what to share and how still may leave you with the challenge of how to integrate these processes into your otherwise busy life. We address that next.
9	**How to Find the Time & Energy to Share** This whole chapter is about taking tiny actions instead of being burdened by big plans. I talk about how to integrate creating and sharing into your otherwise busy life. We will take small actions and turn them into powerful habits. I dig into taking control of your attention and managing your calendar to find time/energy to create, and begin to talk about systems to do so.	You will know how to integrate sharing and creativity it into your otherwise busy life.	Now that they have strategies and systems to share, they have to stay motivated by developing small ways to create momentum and success around their work.

	POINT	OUTCOME	BECAUSE OF THAT . . .
CH.	*Why is this chapter here? What is the experience of the reader in this chapter?*	*What will reader know or feel or be doing by the end of the chapter? Where are they on the journey?*	*How is this chapter connected to the next one? What is the idea that moves the reader from this chapter to the next?*
10	**Find Minimum Viable Success** Here we outline what the simplest version of success with your craft looks like and then we talk about how to get there. We look at how to reframe goals, learn how to measure incremental progress, and develop a system to create and share in small cycles. This addresses the issue that holds too many creators back . . . slowly working towards this "huge launch" that never happens. Or if it does, it never lives up to their expectations, so they stop creating and feel shame.	You will know how to track progress in a way that feels meaningful and accessible, instead of only focusing on traditional markers of success that often let us down.	Too often, people measure the wrong things when judging progress. Next we have to reframe what success looks like when you share.
11	**Measure the Meaning, Not the Numbers** Writers and artists measure the wrong things in this process, and the result is often that they feel bad about themselves. Here we do the opposite: we identify the things that truly matter in terms of how what you create can change people's lives, and also grow your platform and career, exposing your work to more and more people.	You will no longer be controlled by the fear that most people have in sharing their work with others. Instead, we will reframe the act of sharing as one filled with empathy, authentic connection, and support.	The reader is now ready to share their work in a manner that feels authentic to who they are, connected to why they create, and with a system that is both sustainable and flexible. But what's more: they have a better understanding of who they are and a sense of fulfillment and meaning in the process.

TAKE ACTION

- Turn your Table of Contents into an Outcome Outline.

- Use the Seven Point Outcome Outline Checklist to identify holes in the "because of that" logic that connects one chapter to the next. Be brutally honest about what works and what doesn't. You want your Outcome Outline to show a clear transformation journey from beginning to end. You want to feel and see the narrative drive.

- Fix any holes in logic. Sometimes reading the third column out loud allows you to hear the elements that don't make sense.

- If you change something in the Outcome Outline so that it makes more sense, go back and revise any elements in the *Blueprint* that are impacted. If, for example, you combine two chapters, make sure your TOC reflects that change. If you land on a more nuanced way of describing your point, make the change in your answer to *Blueprint Step #2*. You want your *Blueprint* to contain your most up-to-date thinking.

Write Book Jacket Copy

You've now done all of the work you need to do to define and shape your book idea. You should be able to envision it in your mind—to imagine it finished, published, and in reader's hands. So let's go there!

Imagine your ideal reader is in the bookstore. They pick up your book from the one shelf where it sits and read the back jacket. How do you convince them to open it, put it in their shopping basket, and plunk down $25 for it?

Book jacket copy is sales copy. It's meant to entice and draw the reader in, so the language might be a little overblown, a little over the top. Don't be afraid to go big here.

Effective book jacket copy answers six key questions—which are the questions you have just spent time hammering out throughout your work on the *Blueprint*:

- Who is the book for?

- Why do they need it?

- What transformation does it promise?

- What structure does it use to lead the reader through this transformation?

- What is the takeaway/point?

- Why are you the best person to write this book?

What's not on this list?

- Long, drawn-out explanations

- Vague language

- A hit parade of every element you cover in the book

- A full biography of the author

- A defensive, off-putting, or apologetic tone

You can get inspired by studying the jacket copy from your favorite books, but I'll break down two successful examples from my clients (with my comments in bold) to give you some guidance on what to aim for:

CASE STUDY #1

Book Jacket Copy for *The Next Happy: Let Go of the Life You Planned and Find a New Way Forward* by Tracey Cleantis

Every single agent and publisher who heard Tracey's pitch at a conference asked to see her proposal. She landed an agent three weeks later and sold the book to Hazelden in a two-book deal.

Note that Tracey pitched her book with a different title than the one that ended up on the published book.

This copy starts with a timely (at the time), catchy "hook" to lure the reader in—the author was pitching her book two weeks after Jennifer Lawrence won the Oscar for her role in *Silver Linings Playbook*.

In the movie *Silver Linings Playbook*, Jennifer Lawrence's character was at rock bottom. Her dream of a happy marriage, a stable job, and a wholesome reputation was gone. Dead. Over.

Now the author explains exactly who the book is for.

It's a dark place many people often find themselves, but they don't have the benefit of a handsome co-star and a clever script to rescue them. Enter *The Other Side of Impossible: How to Let Go of the Life You Planned and Find the Happy Ending*.

Next, she explains exactly what the book is about. Her explanation is specific, engaging, concise, and enticing.

This book is a place where readers can come when they are done trying or there is simply no more trying to be done. You thought your marriage would last forever? You thought you were going to be a mother? You were sure you were going to be an actor? For years you believed that if you just tried hard enough and hoped and prayed enough that it would all work out the way you wanted it to—only it didn't. The dream is dead and you are left with nothing but a grief that doesn't have a name—or a weekly support group. *The Other Side of Impossible: How to Let Go of the Life You Planned and Find the Happy Ending* is a roadmap through grief and letting go to the other side of the impossible dream, where unexpected happiness waits.

Here the author talks about why she has the authority to write this book, and gives a final, punchy finish to what the book will do for the reader.

> Using my own experience with infertility, my expertise as a psychotherapist, and the examples of accessible archetypal images such as Rudolph the Red-Nosed Reindeer and the Wonder Boys, I give people who didn't get the Hollywood ending a REAL silver linings playbook for moving on.

CASE STUDY #2
Book Jacket Copy for *The Divorce Hacker's Guide to Untying the Knot* by Ann Grant

The first agent who got this pitch responded within three minutes. Ann ended up signing with an agent who loved the book and wanted to be part of the revolution. The book was published with this same title.

This starts with a very compelling set-up about a culture phenomenon that impacts Ann's ideal reader.

> A multibillion-dollar industry has been built around taking advantage of couples who are going through divorce, but the system is rigged. Divorce "professionals" (lawyers, mediators, forensic accountants, and therapists) bill by the hour. They financially benefit when you are indecisive and uninformed. Divorces often needlessly drag on for years, while the "professionals" line their pockets.

Now we get a sense of the author's background that makes her uniquely qualified to write this book.

> I know this story from both sides of the negotiating table. I experienced a high-conflict divorce myself and now run a family-law practice focused on helping women navigate the legal minefields and outsmart the system so they can get to a new life with their sanity intact and their money where it belongs: in the bank.

The jacket copy ends with a clear sense of what's in the book and how it will impact the reader.

> *The Divorce Hacker's Guide to Untying the Knot* gives you this same insider information. It provides strategic guidance concerning the law, finances, real estate, custody, work life, and survival strategies for wellbeing. I show you how to get what you need, let go of what is not working, avoid common pitfalls, and create a new and better life. It's a powerful system to achieve necessary change and take charge of your future, so that you can thrive.

TAKE ACTION

- Write jacket copy for your book. Aim for about 250 words.
- You want to *love* the book you are describing and feel excited to write it and to bring it out to the world. If you don't, keep working on the *Blueprint* until you do.

Conclusion

Congratulations! You've finished your *Blueprint*, which means you've done the hardest work of writing the book. This means that you should be able to visualize it with utmost clarity—where it sits on the bookstore shelf, who is likely to buy it and love it and recommend it, what they will learn from it, and what impact it will have on them.

If you can visualize it, you can write it—and you will find that the writing is so much easier than it would have been if you didn't have this strong foundation. When you sit down to write a section or a chapter, you know exactly why it's there, what it needs to do, and how it connects to the whole.

Of course, you still need to sit down and actually do the work of writing, which demands commitment, habit, and discipline. When the going gets hard—and it will—look back at your why to tap into your deep-level motivation, and let it propel you forward.

The work you have done in the *Blueprint* also sets you up beautifully to develop a book proposal, which is what we will work on next in Part 4.

PART 4

· · · · · ·

Developing a Book Proposal

Many writers new to publishing believe that you write the book and then shop it around to find an agent and a publisher. In truth, most nonfiction books (memoir excluded) are pitched before the book is written. A book proposal is the tool you use to make that pitch. It is an argument for your idea, a business case for your project, a showcase of your expertise, and a declaration of your voice. You use the proposal to invite an agent to represent you and your work.

If an agent decides to offer you representation, you will sign a contract with them. They will then pitch your proposal to acquisition editors at publishing houses. The same proposal is used for both stages of pitching, although your agent will almost certainly suggest tweaking or revising it before they send it out.

Acquisition editors are looking for books the company wants to invest in and publish. At traditional publishing houses, this usually means books that will have a wide, national readership. Small presses, academic presses, and hybrid publishers often acquire books for more niche markets. If you get an offer from a traditional publisher, it will be for a certain amount of money—an advance against sales. You will also be given a delivery date for the manuscript, and part of the money is held back until you write and finish the book.

A lot is riding on your book proposal, and you want to make sure you write a stellar one. The work you have done on the *Blueprint* ensures that you have the solid foundation you need to do that. You've answered all the hard questions; now you need to sell your big idea.

There are eight main elements that agents and acquisition editors expect to see in a proposal, and this order is typical:

1. Overview
2. Manuscript Specifications
3. Author Bio and Photo
4. Audience Analysis
5. Comparable Titles
6. Marketing Plan
7. Annotated Table of Contents
8. Sample Chapters

The following chapters guide you through these elements one at a time to discuss their purpose and how you can turn the material you developed in your *Blueprint* into a great proposal.

Overview

The Overview is a summary of your book. It's the first thing agents and editors read, and it needs to show the entire sweep of the book—who it's for, the problem it's solving, the content it covers, how you have structured it, and why you are the best person to write it. You will pull from many elements of the *Blueprint* to develop your overview. It should be concise—just two or three pages—and its job is to convince agents and editors about the viability of your project; readers will never see it.

Follow these steps to develop a great overview:

1. **Start with a few lines about** the big picture problem your book is solving. What's your point and why is it relevant to the marketplace right now?

2. **Explain who your ideal reader is and why they need the solution you are offering.**

3. **Show the size of your audience and why they need this book now.**

4. **State why you are the best person to write the book.** This is not the place for a full-blown bio, but you do want to claim your authority and establish credibility.

5. **Show the transformation you are promising. Refer back to *Blueprint Step #7* and address the external change and the internal change.**

6. **Explain the structure of the book.** Use phrases like:

   - "In 43 short chapters..."

   - "With 12 quizzes per section..."

   - "Alternating between my own story and stories from other survivors..."

   - "Each of 18 chapters begins with an interview and ends with a checklist...."

These elements do not need to appear in any particular order. You want the Overview to entice and convince, so present the material in whichever order best achieves that goal. In the following two examples, I call out each of the elements.

> **PRO TIP:** *The standard practice when it comes to book proposals is to write in present tense. In terms of whether to write in first person ("This book dives deep into the research I conducted over the last three years") or third person ("This book is about how small business owners can learn the steps to increasing revenue"), there is no hard and fast rule. First person can feel more natural and also lends itself to establishing credibility and authority. You can say, for example, "In my consulting practice, I consistently found..." That being said, the goal of the Overview is to convince the agent and editor on the commercial viability and timeliness*

of the book idea, not only that you have credibility as an author; whatever works best to sell your project is what you should do. Note that the Author Bio (which we'll get to in a moment) is always written in third person as if it were a press release.

CASE STUDY #1
Overview for *The Taste of Opportunity: How to Have a Big Career in the World of Food* by Renee Guilbault

The problem, the context. Why this book matters now.

While there are hundreds of cookbooks published each season, and there are always books about food celebrities, there are seldom books about making a *career* in the world of food. Most people in the food world are not famous chefs with sharp knives and sharp tongues. It's a trillion-dollar industry in America, and it is filled with many different kinds of people, most of whom actually started in a restaurant as a first job. It is often overlooked and underestimated as a real career choice for many reasons, but the food world, and particularly the restaurant industry, is wild with opportunity. It's basically the biggest open career secret in the world. And while Chefs are the obvious, sexy, sassy draw to peeking under the hood, there are so many other roles and fierce opportunities to consider—especially for the generation waking up to life in the adult world and wondering what career paths to follow; for people navigating stalled or derailed careers in industries that destabilized due to COVID; and for anyone ready to make a global impact through the work they do. *The Taste of Opportunity: How to Have a Big Career in the World of Food* is an invitation to come be a part of it, an insider's guide to know how to navigate it, and a challenge to step up and lead it.

The food world is massive. The projected restaurant sales for 2020 were set to be just shy of *900 billion* dollars in the US alone, before the world got turned upside down with COVID-19. With a huge industry rebound on the horizon, the food world is poised to push past pre-COVID levels at any second, not only because it is the third largest expense after Housing and Transportation in American households, but because everybody has to eat, and pretty much everybody in the world loves food—more now than ever before. Who among us hasn't missed the simple pleasure of gathering and sharing food and conversation over a few hours? We all have a renewed appreciation for the enduring significance of food and the many roles it plays in our lives: connection, love, survival, and the joy and memories wrapped around all of it, and this means that there is big opportunity just waiting for anyone to seize it.

Ideal reader

And I mean *anyone*. Most exciting about the world of food is that formal education does not matter nearly as much as how you show up to do your job every day. The keys to a successful career in this business are your talent, discipline, hospitality, warmth, ability to follow directions, and simply being a person who is easy to work with and who keeps your agreements. There are no barriers to achieving incredible things and earning a really comfortable income—it's all up to the individual, what they want for themselves, and if they are willing to do the work to get there. It's one of the reasons I love this industry so much. *There is room in it for everyone from any walk of life who wants to be part of it.* According to the National Restaurant Association, restaurants employ more women and minority managers than any other industry. And nine out of ten restaurant managers started in entry-level positions, which means this is one of the few industries where you can learn on the job and earn your way into a leadership role, regardless of your background or educational achievements. I am here to help anyone find their way who wants a career that is soul-filling, lucrative, and satisfying.

Why the author is the best person to write the book

Why ask me? I am a high school dropout, and I have worked in the food industry since I was 17 years old. Family circumstances meant that it was a better choice for me to leave school and make it out in the world on my own, so the 11th grade is as far as I got in terms of traditional education. No one in my life thought the food world was even a viable career option when I was starting out. I mean people were brutal about it. Dead end jobs, low wages, no career opportunities... yada yada yada... Boy were they wrong!! I had to work my way up in the world with only a few tools— street smarts, my curious and stubborn character, and my own two hands. As I discovered the food world, it took my breath away—it was robust and dynamic, it allowed me to live my life in full color, it didn't care about my flaws, my inner Bridget Jones, or my lack of a diploma, and it had opportunities exploding out of every corner if I was brave enough to take the leap and willing to do the hard work.

After several years of working and discovering the industry (age: 25), I realized that I wanted to become a "real" Chef, so I headed to Paris and obtained my culinary diploma from Le Cordon Bleu, and basically started all over—*again*.

I mean, yes, some of the jobs I have had were just wild, like catering for the porn industry (another book, another time), and others were so obscure (who knew you could oversee food for a global investment bank?), yet I ended up having a long and rewarding career in the world of food FAR beyond my wildest dreams—running restaurants, developing recipes served all over the globe, and travelling the world. As I worked my way up the ranks, I ended up directing the food and beverage platforms for two major international food brands—Pret A Manger in the US and Le Pain Quotidien's Master Franchise globally. I went from running a kitchen of 10 employees in my first kitchen management role to overseeing 1200+ employees in an operation with 40+ restaurants and serving over 70,000 meals a day at Google. Now, I run a consulting company to help other food organizations achieve their goals, so I know exactly what trips people up, what skills and mindset shifts they need, and what it takes to run successful businesses, grow a career, and climb the ladder.

What is the benefit for the reader?

My entire life's story is wrapped around the gracious, open arms of the food world, and I found my forever home here. After all, food is love, connection, humor, and a place where you can actually taste your life in the form of physical memories that can be revisited at anytime, anywhere. It changed my life, and I will always be eternally grateful for the wild and precious ride. It has become important to me to share my experiences and learnings from the ground up, so that others can benefit from my hard knocks, failures, and successes as they look for ways to navigate their own career path. I plan to crack it open for the world to see and share just how incredible this industry is, and how, regardless of your personal imperfections, or your lack of traditional education or background, you can achieve anything you set your mind to. It is finally time for the world to appreciate the food industry for the joy and opportunity it brings to the lives of so many, not just the myriad things that are wrong with it and need fixing.

How the book is structured

The Taste of Opportunity: How to Have a Big Career in the World of Food is not a how-to, textbook, or manual, but rather a real-life view of what to expect from a career in the food business at three distinct levels, plus a look at the some of the global, world-changing, social, and environmental issues you can impact if you make it to industry leadership. I wear different narration hats throughout the book—speaking as a veteran food world executive who loves my industry, a behind-the-scenes insider who knows how things work and how they often don't, a critic of things that are deeply wrong about the food industry, a career coach, a Chef, a sustainable food advocate, and a mom. As a multi-unit manager and an executive, I read every leadership book I could get my hands on, but I wished I had one targeted for the food world specifically. This book will be the go-to manifesto for making your mark on the food world. It includes *stories* that will take you inside kitchens and corporations; a *management mise en place* to show you what tools, skills, and mindsets you need to succeed at each level of this industry; *recipes* that help tell the tale; and a call-to-action for those of us who stay in the business, because once you become a leader in food, you really can change the world.

CASE STUDY #2
Overview for *Compose Yourself: The Essential History of Musical Women Who Broke the Silence and Dazzled Their World* by Susanne Dunlap

The problem, the context. Why this book matters now.

Books that offer a skewed view of history can have a subtle influence on the expectations and aspirations of young girls. A case in point was that when I was three, if someone asked me what I wanted to be when I grew up, I would say Mozart. I wanted to make beautiful music and perform in front of princesses and queens, and my favorite storybook, *Mozart the Wonder Boy,* taught me that such a life as an adult was only available to boys. Girls—like Mozart's talented sister Nannerl—stayed home and helped their mothers keep house.

Why the author is the best person to write the book

As I went on to become quite a serious pianist through high school and college, I never questioned that early lesson, accepting simply as fact that all the great composers were men. The standard piano repertoire consisted of Mozart (of course), along with Beethoven, Schubert, Brahms, and so on; orchestra concerts never, to my recollection, featured anything but music composed by males.

It wasn't until I started graduate school in music history—first earning an MA at Smith College, then a PhD at Yale—that I learned that women were not merely shadowy figures supporting great men, but that many of them were superb composers in their own right. I at last became acquainted with Hildegard of Bingen, Francesca Caccini, Fanny Mendelssohn Hensel, Clara Schumann, and many others. That was in part because by the time I was in graduate school, their music had been "rediscovered." It began to be featured on some recordings and programmed in small performances, and Hensel and Schumann's piano works were available in authoritative editions for pianists like me to play.

But that was confined mostly to the rarefied world of music scholarship. Few who teach music to young people today introduce the female along with the male greats in the musical canon. In fact, almost every one of the existing books about classical music geared toward younger readers names only the famous men composers.

How the book is structured

Compose Yourself aims to address that lack. Featuring over 40 of the most famous women composers from the Middle Ages to today, the book places them within their historical and musical contexts in a way that will engage curious young readers. Biographical sketches, illustrations, and multiple informative sidebars featuring historical tidbits enliven every chapter. Sprinkled throughout will be quotes from 21st-century women and nonbinary classical composers with wisdom and insight about their own journeys to composing.

Ideal reader

Compose Yourself will appeal to students from around age 12—when children are starting to participate in school bands and choruses and gaining some proficiency on their instrument or with their voice—to age 18 and beyond—when those who continued their musical studies are becoming more serious about them. And statistics show that the majority of students who stick to participation in music throughout high school are girls. It saddens me to think that so many of those girls may be wholly unaware that there were women as well as men who wrote music they might be able to play or sing.

Secondary audiences

Compose Yourself will also be a valuable resource for music educators—in public schools, private schools, independent studios, music camps, and performing arts programs open to young people. While it is difficult to dig up exact statistics for the number of music students in the U.S., 8 percent of the roughly 27 million students in public middle and high schools participate in band. That's over two million students. In addition, in excess of a hundred thousand private music teachers with different numbers of students belong to national organizations such as NAfME (National Association for Music Education), and there are around

6,500 music clubs throughout the country with members of all ages.

What is the benefit for the reader?

As not only a music historian but a multi-published author of historical fiction, I possess the unique combination of skill and expertise a book like this requires. *Compose Yourself* brings together just about every aspect of my past in music and in literature—my own piano studies, graduate school in musicology, years of working in performing arts nonprofits, and writing historical novels for adults and teens that foreground music in history.

I'm excited to share the stories of remarkable women composers with young readers. I can't wait to be the one who tells them that the earliest woman composer whose music has survived, Hildegard of Bingen, spent 14 years walled up in a single room with one other woman. Having written adult historical fiction that takes place amid the intrigue of Louis XIV's court, I'm itching to reveal that Elizabeth-Claude Jacquet de la Guerre was the pet composer of Louis XIV's notorious mistress, Madame de Montespan. And talk about multi-tasking: Clara Schumann had to support her eight children through music teaching, performing, and composing after her more famous husband ended his days in a mental institution.

What is the takeaway for the reader?

It's important for girls to see themselves represented in history, to recognize that creative avenues are open to them today that weren't for most women of the past. *Compose*

Yourself: The Essential History of Musical Women Who Broke the Silence and Dazzled Their World does for music what other books have done for women in the sciences, women explorers, and women athletes.

Above all, this book is a celebration of perseverance, passion, and persistence in the service of an overwhelming desire to create music. It's a book full of the joy of possibilities that I hope will inspire girls to see that women were involved in the creation of the music they know and love—even if those women aren't yet household names. *Compose Yourself* brings women's contributions to the musical canon into the minds of young readers, who will become adults with a much more comprehensive—and accurate—view of music history.

Why the Overview Matters

You want agents and editors to read the Overview and think, "Wow this sounds compelling and unique and timely! I can't wait to see all the details and see if the author can pull off what they are promising."

TAKE ACTION

- Review your answers to the entire *Blueprint* and soak it all in.
- Draft an overview, making sure you answer these key questions:
  - » What's the big picture problem your book is solving?
  - » Who is your ideal reader and why do they need the solution you are offering?
  - » Why are you the best person to write the book?
  - » What transformation are you promising?
  - » What is the structure of the book?

······································

Manuscript Specifications

This short section of the proposal gives an indication of how long the finished manuscript will be and when you expect to be ready to deliver it to a publisher. The timeframe may vary greatly depending on how much research needs to be done to complete the book, what else you have going on in your life, and how important it is for the book to be published in a timely manner. Manuscript specs are educated guesses, but they give the agents and editors a sense of the scope of the project and your capacity for finishing it.

To determine total word count of your yet-to-be-written book, take the word count of one sample chapter and multiply it by the projected number of chapters.

PRO TIP: *If your book will include illustrations or graphic elements, use the Manuscript Specifications section to explain your vision.*

CASE STUDY #1

A typical example of Manuscript Specifications

The manuscript will be 50,000 words. It will be complete by January 1, [YEAR].

CASE STUDY #2

Manuscript Specifications for *Compose Yourself: The Essential History of Musical Women Who Broke the Silence and Dazzled Their World* by Susanne Dunlap

Word Count: Approximately 80,000 words. 25 chapters plus an Overture (introduction) and a Coda (conclusion), divided into 6 Movements (sections) with brief interludes.

Artwork: Books for this audience demand visual interest in the form of illustrations and graphic elements. One-color printing is acceptable; two-color is preferred; 4-color would be ideal.

Delivery Date: July 1, [YEAR]

Why the Manuscript Specifications Matter

In reading each successive section of the proposal, the viability of your idea and your credibility as the writer should grow in the agents' and publishers' minds. You want agents and publishers to finish reading the Manuscript Specifications and think, "I can visualize the length of this book and know how long it will take the writer to complete it. I feel confident they understand the word count constraints of their category."

TAKE ACTION

- Write out your manuscript specifications.

Author Bio + Photo

Your author bio is not just a recitation of every degree you've earned, every title you've held, and every award you've won. It's not a resume. It is an argument for why you are the best person to write the book you want to write. The author bio is, in other words, a sales tool that shows your credibility, not a declaration of your general awesomeness—although you may, in fact, come across as awesome. You want agents and publishers to see why you are the best person to write this book, how your background will help sell it, and how you are uniquely positioned to be an advocate for it.

In most cases, you should write the author bio in third person—as if someone is writing about you. Only if your book is very personal—if it includes a lot of your own story and is written in first person—does it make more sense to write the bio in first person.

The author bio should be about a page long. You can use the words you wrote in the *Blueprint Step #2* as a starting point to develop it. That step was largely about convincing *yourself*; here you are convincing others.

1. The first line of the bio should relate directly to your book concept and demonstrate why you are the best person to write this book.

   - A physician writing a book about wellness might say, "Dr. Smith is head of Internal Medicine at General Hospital and the architect of a program that has helped 1,000 people reverse their diabetes."

   - An organizational psychologist writing a book about diversity in the workplace might say, "Over the last five years, Jane Smith has convinced 47 Fortune 500 companies to rewrite their diversity policy."

   - A stay-at-home mom writing a book about getting the kids to eat vegetables might say, "Jane Smith is a stay-at-home mom who has befriended every farmer at the farmers' markets in three counties."

2. Add backstory to tell us why this topic matters to you. Think in terms of the thread that connects your experiences to the topic of your book. Tell a story, in other words, don't just list experiences and accolades.

3. Share any awards or honors you have won (if relevant to the book topic), any advanced degrees or titles you might have earned, or any high-level endorsements (e.g., has presented annually at IBM world headquarters, was a featured guest at Esalen Institute, was named top sleep expert by *Parenting* magazine).

4. If you have a robust platform—a large newsletter following, a big social media presence, a popular

podcast, connection to a prominent professional network, a speaking agent, etc.—briefly mention that information here. You will expand on it in the Marketing Plan section.

5. End with something personal.

6. Include author photo. It doesn't have to be a professional photo. A good photo can be taken on your best friend's cellphone if you pay attention to the background and to the lighting. You want a photo that matches the vibe of the book you are writing. If you are writing a serious book about the healthcare crisis, your author photo is going to be more professional than if you are writing a lighthearted book about the best tacos in Los Angeles.

CASE STUDY #1
Andrea Jarrell Author Bio

Andrea crafted this bio to showcase her writing chops, as her book about aging centers on her own story. Instead of focusing on her considerable career success, she skews everything toward her ability to tell a good story.

> Andrea Jarrell is the author of the bestselling debut memoir *I'm the One Who Got Away*, which was nominated for a National Book Critics Circle Award and named one of the Best Indie Books of 2017 by Kirkus Reviews. Earning a star from Kirkus for "Joyce Carol Oates-like prose with a feminist slant," Jarrell's first book made multiple must-read lists ranging from *Redbook* and *Town & Country* to Literary

Hub. *The Today Show* called it "one of the most buzzed about books of Fall 2017."

Heralded as an uncommonly fine writer by Dani Shapiro, Jarrell earned her storytelling chops as a top branding consultant. She is the architect of transformative brand strategies for mission-driven organizations, change-making startups, and universities like Harvard, Yale, and MIT. She's the one the United States Naval Academy called on to craft its multimillion-dollar fundraising campaign and the one NYU chose to brand its new university in Abu Dhabi.

An expert at crafting stories that inspire bonds of affinity, Jarrell believes the best brands call on the values we hold dear, moving our highest selves to act. Her keen ability to combine market realities with empathy and love is the reason her clients are often overcome with emotion when she presents her work. In fact, whether she "makes people cry" is one of her tests of success.

The ability to stir such emotion is also why her "Measure of Desire" essay was selected for the coveted *New York Times* "Modern Love" column and later chosen by "Fear the Walking Dead" actress Kim Dickens to read on the popular Modern Love podcast. Jarrell's essays have also appeared in *Harper's Bazaar,* Literary Hub, Narrative Magazine, The Rumpus, the *Washington Post*, many other sites, journals, and anthologies, as well as several books on brand strategy and fundraising. She earned her B.A. from Scripps College and her M.F.A. in Writing and Literature from Bennington College.

A Los Angeles native, consummate yogi, hopeful student of French, and mother of two, Jarrell is happily married to her husband of thirty years and living in metropolitan

Washington, D.C. Her longevity hero is Satchel Paige who played Major League Baseball until he was nearly 60, decades longer than players today. His secret? He didn't know how old he was.

CASE STUDY #2
Jennifer Noble Author Bio

This bio tells a story about Jennifer's work. You can see thread that weaves through her bio and connects to her book topic, which is about low-income students and the secrets they know about succeeding.

Jennifer Noble, or Dr. Jenn as she is known on social media, is a licensed psychologist with a PhD in Clinical Psychology from the California School of Professional Psychology, who specializes in adolescents and their parents. She is an associate professor of psychology at Pasadena City College, one of the top community colleges in California and #1 for awarding associate degrees to minorities. Dr. Jenn has a private practice providing psychotherapy in Los Angeles where she works with mixed race teens (and their parents), minority teens (and their parents), women of color, and other marginalized groups. Dr. Jenn uses psychology for social justice; her passion is to work toward equality for all marginalized and oppressed people.

Dr. Jenn's recent research, The Invisible Family Project, was developed with the help of research assistants from her community college to take a strength-based understanding of low-income minority families. Where much of the research focuses on the barriers to achievement, mental health and overall functioning of these families, Dr. Jenn and her research assistants wanted to turn away from the "squeaky wheel" focus to discover what makes the other "wheels" run well. Using more than 50 face-to-face interviews with low-income minority students from universities across the country and surveys with these students (and their parents) she investigated the triumphs, worldview, resilience, and unique perspectives that others don't often see. These interviews will be the backbone of the book.

A Black and Tamil Sri Lankan woman, Dr. Jenn has a passion for racial identity formation and advocating for the mixed-race experience and all the complexity it brings, especially in a monoracist society—work she has been doing for more than 20 years. She is an advisory board member and former past president of Multiracial Americans of Southern California (MASC), a nonprofit in Southern California that serves interracial couples, mixed race people, and transracial adoptees. Dr. Jenn has recently launched The Mixed Life Program, an online coaching program and Facebook community for parents of mixed-race children who want to learn how to help foster a healthy mixed-race identity development in their child.

Why the Author Photo + Bio Matter

You want agents and publishers to finish reading the Author Bio + Photo and say, "This author is absolutely the right person to write this book. They are qualified, passionate, and they have the marketplace awareness to connect with readers."

TAKE ACTION

- Write your author bio.
- Have a photo taken that reflects your professional brand.

···

Audience Analysis

The Audience Analysis section of the book proposal provides evidence that there is a wide readership for your book. It's where you show that the ideal reader you identified in the *Blueprint* is part of a large group of potential readers. Traditional publishers are looking to publish books that appeal to a national audience. You need to define who those people are, where they can be found, and why they might be looking for a book like yours at this time. This section typically includes statistics and data on a primary audience and several secondary audiences.

The size of your target audience can be a critical factor in landing a traditional publishing deal; agents and publishers want to know that your audience justifies their investment in your book. If your audience is too small—too niche, they might say—traditional agents and publishers may not be willing to invest in it. You can't change the facts of who you are speaking to, but you can show what you know and convince them that your audience is ready, willing, and eager to buy a book like yours. Agents and publishers might not know your audience as well as you know it, so your job is to inform them.

How big an audience is big enough? In one week in February 2022, Brené Brown's *Atlas of the Heart: Mapping*

Meaningful Connection and the Language of Human Experience, sold 15,849 copies. Year to date (meaning about six weeks), it had sold 127,195. Brené Brown is a superstar author with many bestselling books to her name. A book further down the list of that same week, *Miss Independent: A Simple 12-Step Plan to Start Investing and Grow Your Own Wealth* by Nicole Lapin, sold 4,817 and had sold 17,060 year-to-date. Those numbers give you a sense of the kind of books traditional publishers are looking to get behind.

Here's another way of looking at it, from agent Steve Laube in 2019:

> "One publisher told me they wouldn't consider publishing a book unless it can generate $250,000 in net revenue in its first year. If a paperback book retails for $15.99 and the publisher receives a net of $8.00 per book, then this publisher is saying that they have a threshold of 30,000 copies in projected sales before they consider publishing a book."

PRO TIP: *If you don't believe your audience is large enough to interest a traditional publisher, that might be a good reason to consider other kinds of publishers. There are fantastic small and mid-level publishers, regional publishers, academic publishers, and hybrid publishers. You may not need an agent to approach other publishers (consult the submission guidelines on their websites) and these kinds of publishers may be a better alignment for your project overall. There is no harm in trying first to land an agent and a traditional publishing deal, as long as you are sending out an excellent proposal to appropriate agents.*

To develop your Audience Analysis, do the following:

1. Start with a short introduction discussing the audience in general, providing context for their interest in your book idea. Note any trends—Is this a growing audience? How do you know?

2. Add more specific information in the form of statistics. Find a respected national organization that compiles that kind of information and get the most up-to-date numbers.

3. If there are other audiences besides the primary one, complete these two steps for the secondary audiences as well. Usually, the primary and secondary audiences are connected by the point of your book. For example:

   • A book about helping women through divorce might also appeal to attorneys or therapists.

   • A book about helping parents learn how to teach their kids better social-emotional skills might also appeal to schoolteachers and school principals.

   • A book about establishing a strong corporate culture that is written for C-suite executives might also appeal to entrepreneurs who want to establish a culture from the ground up.

CASE STUDY #1
**Audience Analysis for *Moms Moving On: Real Life Advice
on Conquering Divorce, Co-Parenting Through Conflict,
and Becoming Your Best Self***
by Michelle Dempsey-Multack MS, CDS

Michelle pitched her book at a time when she had more than
64,000 followers on Instagram and was part of a co-parenting
app with 30,000 subscribers. She had a robust platform, but a
platform doesn't always translate to book sales. Michelle had
to make sure agents and publishers saw that she could reach a
broad audience of dedicated potential book buyers.

My primary audience is a 30-something mother who is in
the process of divorcing. This is a large and needy audience:

- As of the end of 2019, the divorce rate was up to 2.9
  per 1000 population. There were around 800,000
  divorces finalized in that year, which doesn't count
  the thousands of people who have chosen to remain
  separated or who are still in the process of divorcing.

- And in 2020? According to Legal Templates (a company that provides legal documents) the number of
  people seeking a divorce increased 34 percent from
  March–June 2020 compared to March–June 2019.
  Twenty-one percent of couples admit that the lock-
  down was to blame for their divorce.

- The average age for people going through a divorce
  for the first time is 30 years old. According to a recent
  report, more than half, or 60 percent, of divorces
  involve spouses who are between the ages of 25 and 39.

- This, by the way, means a lot of moms with young kids. In 2014, there were 13.4 million parents who were sharing time with an ex, aka co-parenting. Five out of six custodial parents are mothers.

Statistics aside, there is no denying the emotional toll a divorce can take on a mom's life. My reader's life was just blown to bits by divorce. She worries that she'll never be able to rebuild the pieces. She stresses about having to co-parent with someone who treated her horribly. She wonders if she'll die alone or if there truly is a way to be happy after divorce. More than anything in the world, she wants to know it'll all be okay. She wants to know how to tackle problems as they arise instead of drowning in them.

Secondary Audiences

- **Not-yet-divorced women.** A large number of the women I hear from or who want to hire me as a coach are the ones who have been unhappily married for years and are looking for a little push. They want to know what to expect, whether they can handle it, and what life will look like on the other side. They'd feel better taking the leap to better their lives if they just knew what the road ahead was paved with.

- **Women who have been divorced for a long time.** Another audience I have already captured on social media and work within my coaching business is the woman who has been divorced for a while but enjoys the motivation and support that I offer and finds herself having difficulty navigating new stages of co-parenting. She's neglected herself to adjust to life after divorce and is looking to read something that makes her feel seen, understood, and inspired.

- **Divorce attorneys and mediators.** These professionals often reach out to me for resources to help support their clients. I have the benefit of being married to a family court judge and many of his colleagues look to me for support. From these interactions, I know how to target and reach lawyers and divorce specialists all over the country.

CASE STUDY #2
Audience Analysis for *The Taste of Opportunity: How to Have a Big Career in the World of Food* by Renee Guilbault

Unlike Michelle, Renee did not have a large platform or following when she pitched her book, but she knew the audience was enormous. She set about showing exactly how many people could benefit from her book, in very specific ways. In doing so, she also clearly establishes her understanding of the market.

According to the National Restaurant Association, the projected restaurant sales for 2020 were set to be just shy of 900 billion dollars in the US alone, before the world got turned upside down with COVID-19. No one knows how or when the industry will rebound but we all know it will. Not only because it is the third largest expense after Housing and Transportation in American Households (according to the USDA,) but because everybody has to eat. And pretty much everybody in the world loves food.

In pre-COVID times, there were 15.6 million people working in the restaurant industry— about one in 10 working Americans. In 2018, 22.0 million full- and part-time jobs were related to the agricultural and food sectors—11.0 percent of total U.S. employment. The audience for my book lies in specific parts of this universe.

My primary audience is corporate foodservice organizations and their employees. Restaurant companies, food companies, and corporate foodservice providers are my primary audience for several reasons.

- Employee retention, engagement, and development are critical to the profitability and performance of restaurants and yet the restaurant industry employee turnover rate is estimated to be 100 percent + year over year. Turnover is extremely costly and can be brand-damaging due to inconsistent service and guest experience. This book is a much-needed coaching and inspirational tool to help corporate employers explain and highlight the real issues that new and seasoned employees face, and to give them guidance for surviving and thriving.

- The cost per employee turnover is estimated by the National Restaurant Association (NRA) at $2,000 per employee. Those figures will vary by restaurant type since fast-food employees are still less expensive to turn over than those in upscale dining. Key to the effort of retention is to target women and minorities for advancement. Restaurants employ more women and minority managers than any other industry according to the NRA.

- Companies like Panera Bread invest heavily in the early phases of employment: "If people get beyond 90 days, turnover really drops, and so that's why we make investments in technology and training in those first 90 days. It has a huge return," Panera's CFO said. And return matters. In 2017, JAB bought Panera and took the company private for a reported $7.5B deal with over 2,000 locations and 100K employees. Other large food companies like Brinker ($2.9B revenue, +59K employees), Darden ($8.5B +150K employees), Compass Group ($15B USA Revenue, $23B Global Revenue, 600K employees) and Sodexho ($24B Global Revenue, 470K employees) make up a significant market share for investment in retention strategies to keep their employees moving forward and up their corporate ladders.

My secondary audience are Gen Z Workers (aged 15–23 as of 2021) entering the workforce for the first time. [Details omitted for brevity.]

My third audience are employees seeking to move into higher levels of leadership from entry to executive level. [Details omitted for brevity.]

Why the Audience Analysis Matters

You want agents and publishers to finish reading the Audience Analysis and say, "There is a big audience who needs this kind of book, and the author understands the audience well. I can see a clear path for how to sell this book."

TAKE ACTION

- Research your primary target audience.
- Describe the audience and use statistics to back it up.
- Repeat for any secondary audiences.

Comparable Titles

The Comparable Title section of a proposal is designed to provide context for your book in the marketplace. In the *Blueprint*, you decided where your book would sit on the bookstore shelf, and you made a list of the other books your ideal reader is already reading. Now you want to take that list and dig into why your ideal reader loves each of those books, what the books lack, and what your book adds to the conversation.

The goal is to feature approximately five comparable titles in the proposal. Play around with the titles on your *Blueprint* list to find a mix that makes sense. The books you select tell a story and make an argument for why your book belongs on the shelf, for which shelf it belongs on, and for why your ideal readers need it. Only include books that have been published in the last two years.

> **PRO TIP:** *Try not to find the five top selling books in your category, slap them down, and call this job done. A more nuanced approach shows a better understanding of your ideal reader and your audience. Readers*

don't read only the bestselling books in the topic they are interested in. Think about a Venn diagram, with your book in the middle. What are the circles of books that touch on it?

1. Start with a one- or two-paragraph introduction. It should take a 30,000-foot view of the book's place in the universe. It's the same thing that often happens in the opening credits of a movie: a camera pans across a city skyline and then zooms into a particular location. You can refer to the audience you have just analyzed, and to anything going on in the cultural zeitgeist that is critical to know, and then zero in on why your book is a necessary addition to that landscape. This can be a smart place to talk about the big sellers in the category, or to dismiss a book that is an elephant in the room. I had a client, for example, who wrote a book about grief. Comparing her book to the 1969 classic, *On Death and Dying* by Elizabeth Kubler-Ross, doesn't help an agent or editor put a new book in context. But referring to the Kubler-Ross book in an introduction to the section takes it off the table, shows a certain humbleness, and allows the author to use her comp titles in a more efficient way.

2. Write up a short paragraph about each comparable title based on this material. Answer the following questions:

   - How is your book similar?
   - How is it different?

- If you had to tell someone why they should buy your book instead of this book, what would you say?
- If you had to tell someone why they should buy your book in addition to this book, what would you say?
- How can your book be part of the conversation that this book is already having with readers?

CASE STUDY #1

Comp Titles for *The Taste of Opportunity: How to Have a Big Career in the World of Food* by Renee Guilbault

This is one of my favorite comp title section intros because Renee puts her book in a context that is bigger than food books, which is a core tenet of her philosophy.

> There are hundreds of books about food each season—how to buy food, prepare it, present it, and enjoy it. There are also always books about food celebrities—the chefs and restauranteurs in the limelight who teach us, feed us, and inspire us with their personal styles, hero journeys, and stories. *The Taste of Opportunity* is a book about food, but it does not fit into either of the above categories. It's a book about making a *career* in the world of food, all wrapped around personal experiences and learnings, and why ultimately the food world has been such an amazing place to grow up and learn, but it's not as straightforward as a typical career book such as *Designing Your Life* because it's about food and as we all know, food is never straightforward.
>
> And while everyone loves the stories about Chefs becoming Chefs, most people in the food world aren't

Chefs. So much information and experience are missing from the conversation, which drives me nuts! The lack of mainstream books about the wonderful, beautiful things the food world has to offer and how significant it is in most people's lives as either a step into the working world or a career home is an open, gaping wound to me. Most books about the industry call attention to what's wrong with it, but seldomly if ever, are there books celebrating the incredible opportunities the food industry provides to people from all walks of life regardless of education or background.

The book that comes to mind that is closest to what I am trying to do is the moving book about the joys and merits of skilled manual labor, *Shop Class as Soul Craft* by Matthew B. Crawford. The idea that some people are more suited to doing than to thinking was revolutionary, and these are the people who often land in the food world. These are the people I am writing for. I am saying, *Come do this work that lets you "live concretely in an abstract world," as Crawford says. It is a joyful world, a lucrative world, a wonderful world, and I will show you why.* I also think of *The Devil Wears Prada*—a novel about a young woman making her way in the fashion industry and showing us what that world is really like and why that world matters.

But back to food books. Here are five that make the most sense as comp titles:

1. *Kitchen Confidential* by Anthony Bourdain (Ecco, anniversary issue, 2018). Bourdain cracked open the kitchen to teach us what it was REALLY like to work in food. His book is bawdy, his manner is a little crazy, and he comes across as a maverick. It's obviously compelling reading and has led countless

people to want to be a Chef. But not everyone is cut out to be a Chef or wants that job—but they want to work in the world of food. I am trying to invite my reader into an industry filled with possibility and to show them how it can work for them, not just hoping to seduce them with antics.

2. *Culinary Careers: How to Get Your Dream Job in Food with Advice from Top Culinary Professionals* by Rick Smilow and Anne E. McBride (Clarkson Potter, 2010). Although ten years old, this was a clever idea to introduce people to the world of food through 80+ interviews of industry professionals. It serves as an introduction to the world—a buffet of possible jobs, lists of culinary schools—and functions as a "how-to" for culinary enthusiasts to find their way, whereas my book talks about the skills, leadership qualities, and mindset needed to thrive and succeed and takes the reader inside jobs outside of the kitchen and at different levels of management. Additionally, my book is positioned to inspire and motivate, through making what's possible actually achievable at every level of the industry.

3. *Burn the Place: A Memoir* by Liana Regan (Agate Publishing, 2019). This memoir is an exceptionally beautiful, memorable, and unique story of one woman's rise to the top heights of the food world while struggling with addiction and gender issues. It shows what it takes to succeed and offers a raw and poignant inside look, but like many other Chef memoirs, it is a personal story of triumph in the kitchen and running an acclaimed restaurant and does not

look outward to inspire others to join this world. My book is meant to help folks who want a career in food find their way. I provide insight and tips through the sharing of experiences and learnings at every level of the career ladder, and I encourage readers to stay in the industry and unlock their dreams.

4. *Blood, Bones & Butter: The Inadvertent Education of a Reluctant Chef* by Gabrielle Hamilton (Random House, 2012). This book was a ground-breaking memoir about a female chef navigating her place in a man's culinary world. While it is an absolutely brilliant book and so beautifully written, it is a narrow way of looking at the food world, again, from the lens of a Chef and Restauranteur, and doesn't invite people in who might aspire to other paths in the food industry.

5. *Save Me the Plums: My Gourmet Memoir* by Ruth Reichl (Random House, 2019). Reichl is a writer and storyteller and a food lover, but the reason I chose her book as a comp is because she took us inside a part of the food world we had not previously seen— the magazine side. *The Taste of Opportunity* will take readers into many parts of the food world, shining a light into all the places where one can make a career and inspire folks to dream big and stay in it in order to achieve their dreams.

PRO TIP: *The agent who signed Renee for this book felt that her comp titles skewed too strongly toward celebrity memoirs. She understood the reasoning for that choice but felt that a better context for the book were lesser-known books about making a career in other industries. This is the kind of tweaking an agent might suggest you do to your proposal.*

CASE STUDY #2

Comp Titles for *Compose Yourself: The Essential History of Musical Women Who Broke the Silence and Dazzled Their World* by Susanne Dunlap

Compose Yourself belongs to the increasingly well-stocked category of books about women who have been overlooked or underrepresented in history, served up in packages that appeal to young readers who are hungry to see that it wasn't only men who created the world we live in today. While it is pitched to an older group than the bestselling *Rebel Girls* and *Women In...* series, *Compose Yourself* can be seen as the next logical step for readers of these nonfiction books about extraordinary women. Geared toward more sophisticated readers with developing interests in specific topics, *Compose Yourself* provides an in-depth and subject-specific history of women who have mostly been erased from the musical canon. Below are the titles that most closely intersect with the tone, reading level, subject matter, and intent of *Compose Yourself.*

1. *Broad Strokes: 15 Women Who Made Art and Made History (in That Order),* Bridget Quinn (Chronicle, 2017)

   This engagingly written book takes an in-depth and thoughtful look at 15 of the most important women artists in history, starting with Artemisia Gentileschi and ending with Susan O'Malley. Quinn explores not only the biographies of the artists, but also where they fit into the art and society of their times, what they had to overcome in order to become professionals, and society's views of women artists during their lifetimes. Her smart, entertaining text assumes a level of interest and knowledge about the basics of art—very much as *Compose Yourself* does with music. It's also beautifully illustrated, both with original art by Susan Congdon and full-color plates of paintings and sculptures by the featured artists. *Compose Yourself* also takes readers through history from even further back and enlarges the canvas by featuring more over 40 women composers.

2. *A Thousand Sisters: The Heroic Airwomen of the Soviet Union in WWII,* Elizabeth Wein (Balzer + Bray, 2019)

   While this book tackles a very different group of women in a particular era, it takes an analogous approach to *Compose Yourself* in that it provides rich background and context for the stories of the different airwomen profiled. As I do in *Compose Yourself,* Wein situates her subjects in their milieu, delving into Communism and the political philosophy of the time that placed men and women on an equal footing politically and professionally. She also addresses some of the more technical aspects of flying planes in a war. The book uses archival photographs and sidebars to add visual interest, as well as maps.

3. *The Book of Awesome Women: Boundary Breakers, Freedom Fighters, Sheroes and Female Firsts,* Becca Anderson (Mango, 2017)

This broad collection of biographies about women ranges through scientists, politicians, and creative artists in an eclectic mix of topics that races through time and place. Anderson's snappy voice brings the women to life. However, her section on women musicians concentrates on 20th and 21st-century icons—from Big Mama Thornton to Aretha Franklin to Joni Mitchell. *Compose Yourself* is first and foremost a history of classical rather than popular music (although several of the women composers featured achieved popular success during their lifetimes). In addition, rather than being simply biographical, *Compose Yourself* delves into musical style and conventions of the time, assuming at least that level of interest in potential readers.

4. *Symphony for the City of the Dead: Dmitri Shostakovich and the Siege of Leningrad,* M.T. Anderson (Candlewick, 2017)

Anderson's bestselling book brings the story of Shostakovich's Seventh Symphony, written while the composer was trapped in Leningrad while it was under intense fire in World War II, to breathtaking life. Yet the nail-biting excitement of Shostakovich's ordeal is only one aspect of this finely crafted book for teens and young adults. Anderson takes care to ground the story in the history of Leningrad and in Shostakovich's own history and background, taking it beyond a narrative of a particular event to reveal its significance in a broader sense. *Compose Yourself* similarly takes a historical and sociological view of the milieux in which the women composers flourished, with the goal of adding meaningful context to their history.

5. *Teen Trailblazers: 30 Fearless Girls Who Changed the World Before They Were 20,* Jennifer Calvert (Castle Point Books, 2018)

Pitched to a similar audience, this book belongs on the same shelf as *Compose Yourself.* It takes a broad historical view and uses entertaining sidebars and illustrations to draw the reader into the text, which is broken up into digestible bits. It also features a provocative and lighthearted tone, not unlike that of *Compose Yourself,* and doesn't shy away from introducing social and political history. The graphic style is a little younger in appearance than I envision for *Compose Yourself,* but in most other ways it can be seen as in the same category.

Why Comp Titles Matter

You want agents and publishers to finish reading the Comparative Title section and know exactly how to position the book in the marketplace. You want them to say, "I can see this book on the shelf and know just how we will position it."

TAKE ACTION

- Select no more than five books for your comp titles.
- Include the author, publisher, and publication date.
- Put them in reverse chronological order by publication date.
- Craft a paragraph that shows why you are selecting this title, how your book is the same, and how it is different.

....

Annotated Table of Contents

The Annotated TOC needs to describe the *exact* material that will be in the book so that an agent can glance through a few pages and instantly see the structure and content of the book. In the Overview, you capture the whole sweep of it. Now you need to break down that idea into chapters and present a more thorough and detailed picture. This is where you showcase your reader transformation journey.

The Outcome Outline you created in the *Blueprint* will be your foundation for this section, but instead of just one sentence, you can develop full paragraphs to describe each chapter. You still want to preserve the sense of narrative drive and how each chapter is connected to the one that comes before and after it, but you have more room to expand your ideas. You can go into much greater depth and showcase your voice—which is to say your style of writing.

How long should each chapter description be? It depends on how many chapters you have and how dense the material is. The Annotated TOC is normally anywhere from three to eight pages.

CASE STUDY #1
Table of Contents for *Happy Campers: 9 Summer Camp Secrets for Raising Kids Who Become Thriving Adults* by Audrey Monke

These are three of the twelve entries for Audrey's Annotated TOC:

Camp Secret #1: Connection Comes First

Connection is the "why" of camp. Our overarching purpose is for kids to feel included and valued in a supportive, loving community. In order to foster the feelings of acceptance and belonging that lead to connection, counselors focus on developing what we call "REALationships" with campers. To that end, we have developed specific, actionable practices and trained our counselors to implement them. Even campers who are new to camp feel connected almost immediately, and that is why so many kids consider their counselors and camp friends their closest friends, despite only spending two weeks with them. Many campers return summer after summer and refer to camp with words like "home" and "family." Once parents understand the importance of connection, they can implement practices and traditions that foster greater feelings of acceptance and belonging at home.

Camp Secret #2: Positive Practices Produce Optimistic Kids

The positive atmosphere at camp does not happen by chance. Specific research-based practices implemented by counselors train campers' brains to be more cognizant of positive incidents and behaviors and to think more positively about situations and people. This positivity often translates into a more optimistic and hopeful outlook about their challenges, themselves, and their friends. Many campers take this new attitude home with them at the end of their camp stay, with their parents noting the change. Optimism serves as an important buffer and antidote to depression and anxiety—conditions which are on the rise, with a younger and younger age of onset. By replicating aspects of the camp culture of positivity and developing new family habits and practices, parents can boost their kids' optimism at home.

Camp Secret #3: Kids are More Responsible and Capable Than Parents Think They Are

Kids are capable of doing a lot more than what many parents (and subsequently the kids themselves) believe they can do. Being given more and greater responsibilities—especially ones adults have traditionally taken on themselves due to the mistaken belief that kids are "too young" to do them—is what increases kids' competence. At camp, even our youngest campers are expected to take care of their own belongings and are encouraged to take on tasks they've never tried before. At home, parents can step back from doing things for kids and implement these camp practices to increase their kids' level of responsibility to take care of themselves and their environment. Helping kids become responsible and capable ensures a more successful launch into adulthood.

CASE STUDY #2
Table of Contents for *Moms Moving On: Real Life Advice for Conquering Divorce, Finding Confidence, and Moving on to Bigger and Better Things*
by Michelle Dempsey-Multack MS, CDS

These are three of the 28 entries in Michelle's Annotated TOC:

Stage 1: It's Over, Now What?

So, your marriage is over. The well has run dry. The glass is empty. What now? What do you tell people? How do you handle the questions? Should you just jump on the next person who looks your way? Are you better off just crawling into a hole and hibernating until next spring? Oh, but wait, you have kids to take care of, how does that work?

Chapter 1: The 5W's of Breaking the News (Who, What, When, Where, Why and How to Spill the Divorce Beans)

Your grandma won't understand—"he was such a nice boy!" Your neighbors will dig for information, asking if your soon-to-be-ex-husband's car is in the shop for repair when they don't see it in the driveway. The questions will pile in (almost always when you're with your kids) and you'll need a way to keep the inquiries—and your emotions—at bay. Spoiler alert, no one needs to find comfort in your truth but you.

Chapter 2: Pulling Yourself Out of Bed After Reality Sets In

Like waking up from a bad dream, as soon as you're jolted alert by your toddler, reality sets in. You think, I'm alone again. I have to battle motherhood AND a divorce. How the hell am I going to do this? I had this thought each day—until I replaced that question with something a lot more powerful—the fact that I've done hard things before, and I can certainly do them again.

Chapter 3: You're Divorced, Not Dead

"MY LIFE IS OVER" you'll cry to anyone who'll listen. The truth is, though, it's not. You're still breathing—we've just got to shift your perspective. How? By recognizing the good in the bad, the rainbow after the rain, the lemonade to be made from lemons.

Why the Annotated Table of Contents Matters

You want agents and publishers to finish reading the Annotated Table of Contents and understand the entire book. You want them to say, "This author already did all the hard development work on this book. I can see the transformation journey for the reader and I can feel the narrative drive. I can visualize the entire thing and I love it!"

TAKE ACTION

- Start with your Outcome Outline and expand each chapter so that the purpose and the contents is clear.

- Make sure the narrative drive remains solid and that the reader transformation journey is clear.

....

Create a Marketing Plan

Some writers think that their publisher is going to do all the marketing of the book, and while this may have been true back in the day and may still be true for famous writers or those who get big advances, it's no longer typical. Writers have to take the lead on marketing their own books, which means we have to develop a detailed plan—not only for launching the book, but for reaching readers for years to come. The Marketing Plan section of the proposal is your chance to show exactly how you are going to connect with your ideal audience to get them to buy your book.

You will hear agents and publishers talk about the need for writers to build a platform. Having a platform means that you have an existing and captive audience of people who are ready and waiting to buy your book. This obviously minimizes the risk publishers are taking. When James Clear sold *Atomic Habits*, which went on to become a mega bestseller, he had a devoted newsletter readership of 200,000 people. Publishing his book was a far less risky venture than publishing the book of a writer with no following at all. That being said, simply having a large platform, doesn't guarantee a book deal. I have seen people with massive followings fail to attract agents or editors because they didn't do the hard work of defining what their book was or who it was for—that's why we begin with the work of the *Blueprint*.

Platforms can be built in a wide variety of ways. You can write a popular newsletter like Clear did, or develop a strong social media presence, or lead a community that meets online or in person. You can also build a platform by being an in-demand corporate trainer or speaker, or by being a popular professor or consultant, or by becoming a gamer with a devoted following on Discord. While there are certainly TikTok stars who amass huge followings overnight, for most people, building a platform takes time.

How big a platform is big enough isn't only about the size of the numbers but also the quality. For example, an Instagram following of 500,000 absolutely gets agents' and editors' attention, but an engaged mailing list of 10,000 people is equally persuasive since that audience is captive (meaning you can email them directly). And that 10,000-person mailing list is more persuasive than a Twitter following of 10,000 people, because if the writer lets their mailing list know about their book, odds are good a lot of them will open the email and buy it. If the writer tweets about it, however, odds are good that most of the audience won't even see the tweet. Does all this mean you are doomed if you don't already have a platform?

Not at all.

For people who have done original research (e.g., academics or journalists), or built a successful company or a movement from scratch, lack of platform tends to be much less critical to getting a book deal. These kinds of writers have something unique to say and if they can present a clear vision for their book, publishers will likely take a risk on the project.

For everyone else, you need to show that you are highly attuned to your ideal reader—that you know who they are and how they tend to engage with ideas (what podcasts they listen to, what conferences they attend)—and you need to have a specific plan for how to connect with them. It is not enough to say, "All the yoga teachers will love my book," or "I will market this book to moms of young kids." The marketing plan must be very specific to the ideal reader and the stated audience, and it must include actions you are either already taking or are poised to take.

You also want this plan to be realistic and to take advantage of your interests and strengths. If your ideal readers love listening to podcasts but you can't stand the sound of your own voice, building a marketing plan based on podcast appearances makes no sense. If you are terrified of public speaking, you're not going to want to pitch yourself as a conference speaker. If you don't have a robust and active network of connections, you can't leverage it.

How to Build a Marketing Plan

Most marketing plans have somewhere between three and six primary channels. These might include:

- Leading a community or group either online or in-person

- Having a devoted newsletter following

- Teaching your content through courses and webinars

- Speaking at online or in-person conferences and events

- Sharing your ideas on podcasts (your own or other people's)

- Sharing your ideas in articles and guest posts

- Sharing your ideas on radio and television

- Forming partnerships with other people who are reaching your readers

- Leveraging a strong network of connections to spread the word about your work

There are just two simple steps to creating a marketing plan. Simple—but definitely not easy: 1. Identify a channel that will work for you and your ideal reader. 2. Create activities to broadcast in each channel.

Once you've made these decisions, describe very specifically what your plan is going to be:

- If you want to create a community, who will you invite and where will you reach out to them?

- If you plan to build an email list and send a newsletter, where will you post lead magnets, what topics will you cover, and how often will you send out your newsletter?

- If you will be building a course and doing in-person workshops, what's the course? How does it connect to the contents of your book? Where will you be giving it?

- If you are hoping to give speeches, which conferences or events are you targeting, and what would be the title of your breakout or keynote speech?

- If you intend to pitch yourself as a guest on podcasts, which podcasts and what's your pitch?

- If you are planning to write articles, what publications will you target, and what are the headlines of the articles you will pitch to each?

- If you want to be a guest on radio or television, which programs will you target and do you have contacts that make a guest appearance an attainable goal?

- If partnerships are part of your marketing plan, who will you partner with and how will that help you build your audience?

- If you will be leveraging a network of connections, who are they? If you have primary connections with celebrities or experts in your field and you have confirmation they will help you, mention them.

I have chosen to share marketing case studies from two authors who had relatively modest platforms and did a great job of making compelling cases for their books. Influencer marketing plans with their big numbers and long lists of powerful connections tend not to be as instructive.

CASE STUDY #1
Marketing Plan for *Braided: A Journey of Thousand Challahs*
by Beth Ricanati

Note that Beth pitched her book with a different title than the one that ended up on the published book.

Make Challah and Call Me in the Morning targets primarily women, specifically moms. And nationally, women make at least 70 percent of all household decisions—including, importantly here, the purchasing decisions. Thus, this book is really just a stepping stone to a larger effort to build a national community around the simple ideas elaborated on the pages of *Make Challah and Call Me in the Morning:* the need to slow down, the need to be present, the need to connect with others.

The following marketing section outlines ways that I will connect with audiences across the country—in person, online, and in print. *Make Challah and Call Me in the Morning: A Physician's Simple Recipe for Healthy Living* is a book with significant commercial potential because it has a built-in community-gathering component that is ideally suited to book clubs, community events, and media (television, the web, and even radio). I envision making challah everywhere I go, inviting women to get their hands messy in bowls of dough, demonstrating with them new braiding techniques, and breaking bread with each other.

Cooking demonstrations will include the following parts, at a minimum: I will bring the six ingredients and the various tools that are required to make challah. In addition, I will bring a bowl of dough that has already risen. We will mix the ingredients together as I go through my talking points, just like I was making challah in my kitchen on any given Friday. We will then take the bowl of dough that I've brought and learn how to braid with that dough. I will also bring a finished loaf—to taste of course! Depending on the number of attendees and where the event is being held, we will hopefully be able to arrange for the women themselves to participate with enough ingredients to go around.

1. In-person Events and Appearances

- Book Tour. I am already in the midst of planning a 12-city book tour in which I make challah with groups of women in Los Angeles, New York City, San Francisco, Washington, D.C., Portland, Cleveland, Minneapolis, Durham, Chicago, Houston, Miami. In each of these cities, I have secured housing and a promise of at least 20 women in each location. These events will be an opportunity to spread the challah gospel, do media events, and sell books.

- Independent Bookstores. My plan is to partner with independent bookstores in each of these communities (e.g., Diesel in Los Angeles, Powell's in Portland, Politics and Prose in Washington, D.C., The Bookcase in Wayzata). I will approach the stores about providing books for the home-based bread-baking events and will also offer to do in-store events.

- School Book Tour: I plan on taking my show on the road to schools, much the way that Wendy Mogel did with *Blessings of a Skinned Knee*. I will speak to parents about my journey, read excerpts from my book, and bake bread in school kitchens. As part of this tour,

I will also reach out to do community workshops and challah-making events.

- Book Fairs: I will participate in targeted book fairs, such as school book fairs and at food-related book fairs, such as the FoodBookFair in Brooklyn.

2. Print Publications

Short articles highlighting some of the salient themes of *Make Challah and Call Me In the Morning* are great for magazines—both mainstream magazines as well as select specialty magazines (i.e., women's health and food-based). Pitch ideas can be taken from the three overarching themes of the book—slow down, be present, connect with other women—as well as by subtopic from each of the chapters in the book. These topics also resonate well with specific calendar events, i.e., various Jewish holidays, women's health months (i.e., October – breast cancer awareness; February – women and heart disease), Mother's Day, etc. A partial list of pitch ideas from different chapters in *Make Challah and Call Me In the Morning* include:

- Women's Magazines: *More, Elle, Oprah, Family Circle,* etc. Pitch story ideas from various chapters, including "Saved by the Challah," "Rising Up" or "Finding time on Fridays."

- General Interest Magazines: *People, Time, Newsweek, NYT Magazine, Good.* Pitch story ideas from various chapters, including "Kid's challah French toast recipe" or "The First Blessing."

- Women's Health Magazines: *Women's Health, Shape, Self, Prevention.* Pitch ideas from "Doctor's Note."

3. Online Events and Appearances

I will make contact with the following bloggers to take advantage of the thriving online food world, targeting different markets, including challah bloggers, food bloggers, and bloggers who've come to food from some other professional realm, much like I did. I will create pitches for each of these that will be site-specific. These are just examples, by the way; there are hundreds of blogs that will work in each category. Pitch ideas include book giveaways, author Q&A, and short how-to-make-challah videos. The following is a partial list of target sites:

- Specific blogs that I already have a relationship with:

  [Details omitted for brevity.]

- Jewish food blogs: For all of these, I will pitch ideas such as a book review articles as well as author interviews around various Jewish holidays, especially Rosh Hashanah – when we specifically dip challah in honey.

  [Details omitted for brevity.]

- Food blogs: Pitch ideas will include a Q&A about the vilification of white bread, short articles taken from the "In Preparation" section of the book: mis en place, various ingredients, finding time on Friday, etc.

  [Details omitted for brevity.]

- Food/journey blogs: Pitch ideas will include, for example, short stories about the first time making challah, the rituals around both making and eating challah.

  [Details omitted for brevity.]

- Wellness blogs: Pitch ideas will include short stories based on the side bars in the book that focus on wellness and the various ingredients, as well as stories about wellness as related to the three big themes of the book: slowing down, being present, and building community.

  [Details omitted for brevity.]

- News blogs: I will pitch ideas such as a book review article as well as author interviews around various Jewish holidays, especially Rosh Hashanah, as well as around specific calendar events for women, i.e., Breast Cancer awareness in October and Heart health in February.

  [Details omitted for brevity.]

- Lifestyle blogs: I will pitch short book reviews, especially with beautiful photography of the ingredients, making challah, braiding challah, etc.

  [Details omitted for brevity.]

4. Social Media Community Building: Blog/website/Facebook/Instagram:

Social media sites provide an opportunity for this community to grow: women can post pictures of their challah-making endeavors; they can share baking and life tips; they can share the stories behind the people in whose merit they are making bread that week. On the book's website, there will be message board software for readers to build community. These outlets will also have author Q&A.

This book and the ideas within lend itself to Instagram. I have built up an engaged following of almost 4,500 and will not only post on my site but work some of the more engaged followers to help promote the book. In addition, all of the blogs that I have working relationships with now (see above) can promote the book on their Instagram and other social media platforms as well.

I will create short trailers—teasers—to be posted on these sites as well as on YouTube, to advertise the book. These beautifully crafted trailers will feature the process of making challah (the six ingredients, making the dough, braiding the dough, the finished product), women coming together in the kitchen and sharing stories, families eating the bread together. These trailers will include author Q&A.

CASE STUDY #2
Marketing Plan for *Leaf Your Troubles Behind: How to Destress and Grow Happiness Through Plants* by Karen Hugg

This book lends itself to gardening-related and book-related media, both of which I've done in the past. I'm a traditionally published fiction author whose novels feature strange and interesting plants. To promote *The Healing Magic of Plants*, I'm open to any and all promotional opportunities. I have written and published articles, been interviewed on audio and video podcasts, and have appeared on broadcast television. I have taught in the horticultural realm briefly and am open to speaking engagements.

When my novel *The Forgetting Flower* was released, I worked with a publicist to promote my work and am open to again hiring a publicist (in addition to working with one at a publishing house). In fall, 2019, I hired Smith Publicity, an established PR firm in New Jersey, to help me promote *The Forgetting Flower*. We enjoyed a mutually enthusiastic relationship with my publicist and our collaboration led to a lot of strong promotional exposure. I'd be happy to work with Smith again. See below for my article publications, as well as the podcast and television appearances I did during that time.

My Author Platform

Over the last several years, I've established a website, blog, and newsletter. The site, www.karenhugg.com, has 3,700 followers. My monthly newsletter reaches about 500 subscribers. Though this number is small, my audience is very loyal and engaged, often replying to my mails and reviewing books when requested. During 2021, I hope to boost my followers to 4,000 and my newsletter to about 1,000 subscribers via blogging twice a week and related book giveaways and advertising to attract subscribers.

Before this book is published, I'm happy to enter various non-fiction book contests such as the Pacific Northwest Writers' Association contest (of which I've won Third Prize in the fiction category before); the American Writers and Writing Programs contest; Garden Writers Association Awards; and other annual contests. After the book is published, I'm happy to not only enter the book in whatever contests apply but also support my publisher in whatever way I can to ensure the book lands on Netgalley, Publishers Weekly, Library Journal, Booklist, Kirkus Reviews, etc.

Blogs and Websites

Because I've blogged on my website, I'm open to blogging on other sites as well. I've guest posted on *Garden Rant*,

Women's Books, The Globetrotting Gal, The Daily Echo, and others. I've been interviewed for or the subject of an article on smaller book blog sites and local news blogs. I'm open to contacting several gardening bloggers I'm closely acquainted with to see if they're interested in covering the book. *Garden Rant* is the highest profile gardening blog and I've guest posted there before. I'm happy to contact the editors about doing so again.

In terms of websites, I've created my own platform at www.karenhugg.com and have published articles and or been interviewed at *Seattle Met, Crime Reads, Thrive Global, The Big Thrill, Garden Center Magazine, Trip Fiction*, etc. I'm happy to pitch these outlets again.

In terms of article placement, *Garden Center Magazine* is an industry magazine aimed at horticulturalists. I've published an article there and will contact the editors about doing so again. *Thrive Global* publishes lifestyle and wellness articles. I published a personal essay there in 2019 and can contact editors about writing an article on strategies for healing stress through nature and plants. *Psychology Today* is a high-profile psychology magazine and blog. I can pitch an article about plants and mental health there. The *Washington Post* Health section regularly publishes articles on mental health from freelancers and I have a friend who regularly publishes there, whom I can ask for a contact.

Social Media
Before and after the book is published, I intend to regularly run posts related to plants and mental health on all of my social media accounts for word-of-mouth publicity and garner reviews from online friends, colleagues, and fans.

- www.karenhugg.com/twitter, 2,800 followers
- www.facebook.com/karenkhugg, 750 followers
- www.instagram.com/karenhugg, 300 followers
- www.pinterest.com/karenhugg, 360 followers

Radio, Podcasts, TV/Video
As I mentioned, in the last five years I've been interviewed on both gardening-related and book-related podcasts and radio shows. They are *Back to My Garden* (audio), *New Books Network* (audio), *The Urban Farm U* (audio), *The Tom Sumner Show* (radio), *The Reading and Writing Podcast* (audio), *The Hero Within* (audio), *The Happy Writing Podcast* (audio), and *Must-Read Fiction* (video). I can pitch those outlets for interviews.

I've done one broadcast television segment. In October, 2019, I appeared on the television show *New Day Northwest* to talk about spooky houseplants and my novel *The Forgetting Flower*. I'm willing to pitch the producer again. Daytime shows such as this one could be excellent exposure for this book as they often focus on wellness issues and home and garden topics.

I have done in-person book readings before and am open to appearing in public again. When I've appeared before audiences, either at readings or in classes, I've brought humor and energy to the presentation. I can imagine speaking about my concept of Green Leisure to live audiences while demonstrating some of the more craft-oriented activities I recommend in the book. Though I haven't led this type of workshop before, I can also imagine running a hands-on mental health class where I lead a group of people in therapeutically exploring some of the concepts from the book in real time. I have a friend who runs a retreat called Wide Open Writing, and I'm an alum of the Northern California Writer's Retreat. I can also imagine even appearing at writers' conferences. Lastly, I'm open to speaking about the growing body of research about plants and mental health at a gardening show (perhaps in my home city of Seattle at its Flower and Garden Festival or the Portland Home and Garden Show, or San Francisco Flower and Garden Show, etc.).

When my novel *The Forgetting Flower* was published, I received several blurbs from established authors. Among those who praised the book were bestselling authors Emily Carpenter, Deborah Lawrenson, Sue Burke, and Marty Wingate. I have good relationships with all of those authors and Ms. Wingate is a fellow Seattle garden writer who I think would be open to blurbing this book as well. I also have a cordial relationship with Ciscoe Morris, a gardening television expert and author in the Seattle area, who I'd be happy to ask for a blurb. Lastly, though I don't have connections with them, I'm more than willing to ask Florence Williams, Meik Wiking, or even Gretchen Rubin for a foreword or blurb as they are authors who share my worldview.

Lastly, Facebook, Amazon, and Goodreads are powerful tools for book promotion. I've devoted resources to their book ads and giveaways in the past and am happy to do so again. I can see running a pre-order promotion where when people order the book, they receive a small plant or bookmark as a gift. Similarly, for the past three years, I've partnered with Renee's Garden and given away bee-magnet wildflower seed packets to new newsletter subscribers and this has been enormously successful. I can pivot this promotion toward the book as well. After the book is published, I'm happy to run giveaways through the above mediums. I'm also open to partnering with the American Horticulture Society, The Washington State Nursery and Landscape Association, the American Psychological Association, and other non-profit organizations to do a book giveaway or event.

Why the Marketing Plan Matters

You want agents and editors to read your marketing plan and say, "This author knows how to reach their intended audience and the size of that audience makes the book worth my time, effort, and money."

TAKE ACTION

- Select at least three marketing channels you will focus on in your marketing plan. Explain how using this channel will help you reach your readers—why it's a good fit for your audience and for you.

- For each channel, develop specific examples that show how your content will function in that space.

....
Create Sample Chapters

A strong book proposal will include one or two finished, polished sample chapters—somewhere in the neighborhood of 30 pages of double-spaced 12-point text with 1-inch margins. The sample chapters demonstrate your ability to write the compelling, cohesive, well-structured book you have described throughout the proposal.

> **PRO TIP:** *Note that no matter what I recommend, you have to follow the agent's submission guidelines and they are all different. So, if an agent says, "Attach 10 pages," that's what you do, regardless how long the sample chapter is. In this case, you would cut a 15-page chapter off at 10 pages. If they say, "Paste in five pages," you would cut off a 15-page chapter at five pages.*

Choose chapters that showcase your writing ability and your book idea. The introduction or first chapter usually sets the tone for the whole book, and introduces the topic in a coherent way, so it's an appropriate piece to include. Many writers elect to also include Chapter 2 to build their case and show the momentum of the book.

There are some instances where you might want to choose a chapter that appears later in the book. Those might include the following:

- If you are writing a book with any kind of a "back and forth" structure, you may want to showcase all the elements (e.g., different voices or different periods of time).

- If you have a Section 2 or 3 in the book that's very different from Section 1, you may want to include a sample chapter from one of the other sections.

Use your Outcome Outline as a roadmap to guide your sample chapter writing. Make sure your writing captures the purpose and point of the chapter and that the end drives to the next chapter, even if that next chapter is not one of your samples.

Why the Sample Chapters Matter

You want agents and editors to read your sample chapters and say, "I am ready to sign this author for this project! I love everything about it! I'm convinced!"

TAKE ACTION

- Write one or two sample chapters.
- Edit and revise each chapter. Repeat until they are polished to a high shine.

The "Good Enough" Proposal

Some writers rush to finish a proposal and risk rejection with no chance of resubmission. First impressions count, and there are few second chances with agents. Don't submit a rough draft that you know still has a lot of holes and problems. Likewise, don't sign up for an online pitch conference to "test the waters" or go to a conference and throw your hat in the ring to meet with agents if you only finished a first draft of your proposal yesterday. Meet with agents when you have a solid proposal that demonstrates your very best work.

You can also go too far in the other direction. Sometimes writers spend so much time polishing that they never pitch. They work endlessly to polish their work to a high shine—but it's all a front for their crushing self-doubt. They are refusing to let the work go because if they don't let it go, they don't have to risk rejection. The book can live in their minds as whole and sparkling and it never has to go into the world.

When pitching agents, you want to land somewhere in the middle of rushing to pitch and never pitching at all. You want the pitch to be "good enough", a term used by my friend and client KJ Dell'Antonia when she was working on her first novel, *The Chicken Sisters*.

When KJ turned to fiction writing, she was already a very accomplished nonfiction author, essayist, and editor, who spent many years at the *New York Times* editing the Motherlode column. She well understood that the day you hand your manuscript (or proposal) over to your editor is still a long way away from the day the book goes to press. The editor will have thoughts, and the writer and editor will work together to get the story ready for publication. She knew, in other words, that when going out to agents, her manuscript had to be good enough, but not perfect. This is the mark of a pro.

A proposal that is good enough to pitch is *very good*. It's actually *excellent*. It may have been edited and proofed by a professional—a friend in the publishing business or someone you paid. But it doesn't have to be *perfect*. The agent may suggest that you change your proposal. They may suggest that you change it a little—tweaking things here and there, maybe adding a chapter or two. Or they may ask that you change things a *lot,* and you have to decide if you agree with those changes. This is one of the reasons that when an agent offers you representation, you need to remember that you are also vetting *them*. You want to make sure that you share the same vision for the book.

Once you land a publishing deal, the editor may also have changes to suggest to the book. All of this is to say that pitching is not the end of the process of developing your proposal; it's just one stop on the journey.

If you are dragging your feet on pitching and going around and around on the same pages wringing your hands over whether or not they are ready, you might try pitching to a small group of agents to test the waters, and to build your muscle for pitching. Rejection is not fun, but you will survive.

PART 5

• • • • • •

How to Pitch Your Proposal

Literary agents are the gateway between writers and traditional publishers. Now that you have created a proposal for your book, you'll pitch your idea to potential agents who you would like to represent you. This section presents the steps for creating and executing a pitch plan, which includes identifying potential agents, crafting a query letter to pitch to them, and responding to interested agents.

Pitching agents is uncomfortable for almost every writer. You are approaching strangers who have the power to say yes or no to work you have poured your heart into, and you only have one shot. If an agent says no, it's no. That door is closed for good. Most adults don't face the possibility of that kind of stark rejection very often in their business or personal life, so it's an uncomfortable place to be. Just acknowledging the discomfort and the fact that you have so little control can help to mitigate the anxiety of it.

It can also help to realize that pitching is not akin to throwing darts at a board. You will be researching agents, making a strategic plan, and approaching the entire endeavor with intention.

There are smaller boutique, university, and hybrid publishers who accept pitches directly from writers, and if you choose this approach, the process is similar to pitching to agents. I'll talk about that specifically in *How to Pitch Step #6*, but you'll want to be familiar the five steps for pitching to agents all the same.

....
What Kind of Agent Do You Want?

With more than a thousand literary agents in the U.S. alone, the first step in preparing a pitch plan is to determine what kind of agent you want so you can narrow the field as you search for agents to whom you'll pitch your proposal.

A literary agent represents you, your work, and your best interests. You need someone to sell your book, obviously, but an agent is also an advocate, a partner in building your career, and someone you will lean on to understand the business, the industry, and the language of a publishing contract.

Much like finding a lawyer, a doctor, or an accountant, you want an agent who can meet your specific needs. You can find a great agent no matter your requirements. Here are some questions to guide your thinking:

- Do you want a hard-hitting business partner? Someone who is no nonsense? Or do you prefer an agent who is more nurturing in their manner?

- Would you prefer someone who has a slate of big-name authors and big-name editor pals—but who may have an assistant answer their phone? Or do you want to have someone instantly responsive to you? You might better find this in an agent who works for themselves.

- Would you like your agent to have lots of agency associates to handle things such as contracts, film rights, and foreign rights, or is fine with you if they work with subcontractors on these elements of the business?

- All agents do some level of edits before sending your book out to publishers, but there's a broad spectrum of involvement. Do you want an agent who is hands-on or one who is more hands-off?

- Are you willing to sign with a brand-new agent? There's no right or wrong answer here. If they've been an agent a long time, you get their years of experience, but they might have a crammed client list and little time to budget for a new writer, or they might be close to retirement. A new agent, on the other hand, is often hungry to build their list.

- Do you want an agent who works in New York City, which is widely considered the center of the publishing universe, or does that make no difference to you? There are great agents who live all over the U.S.

- Do you want an agent or an agency that represents all the genres you think you might like to write in the future or are you just looking to sell this one book right now?

- Is it important to you that the agent is actively working towards diversity in publishing?

As long as the agent is a professional who represents your genre and is currently open to clients, everything else is a matter of personal preference.

PRO TIP: *Be on alert for red flags, and trust your instincts. Signing an agreement with a literary agent is a legally binding business contract in which you are promising a percentage of your earnings and giving someone the right to represent you in business dealings. You want to make sure the agent you are signing with is reputable. There is an Association of Authors' Representatives, Inc., whose members must meet the highest standards of ethics, and this is a good place to double-check the integrity of the agents you are considering. But membership does not guarantee anything, nor does every excellent and legitimate agent belong to the organization. Some younger agents do not yet qualify for membership, and some legitimate agents choose not to join. The best thing to do to guard against unscrupulous players at agencies is to do a thorough job with your research so that you understand the landscape and can more easily identify problems.*

TAKE ACTION

Check off all the characteristics that are important to you in an agent:

- ☐ Nurturing
- ☐ No nonsense
- ☐ Represents big-name authors
- ☐ Part of a big agency
- ☐ Works for themselves
- ☐ Hands-on editorial
- ☐ Years of experience
- ☐ Works in New York City
- ☐ Hungry for new clients
- ☐ Actively seeking diversity
- ☐ Represents multiple genres you are interested in writing
- ☐ Other _____

Research Agents

With your agent checklist in hand, you can begin to identify a long and short list of agents you'll pitch. The goal is to have a short list of approximately 10 agents you adore and 20 or more who you really, really like.

This is perhaps the most time-consuming part of your pitch plan because there are so many agents and so many resources to consult. It will likely take multiple passes in a process of elimination to narrow your choices. At the highest level, you want an agent who represents your genre and who is accepting new clients. Once you've identified agents who meet those criteria, you can begin to identify those who have other characteristics you desire.

> **PRO TIP:** Make a spreadsheet to track your research. You especially want to note the agent's submission requirements because each will be different. Some want a query letter and 10 sample pages. Some want a query letter and your Overview. Some want a query letter and the whole proposal. It's easier to track those requirements on a spreadsheet than to return to 30+

websites over and over again to look it up. You can download a spreadsheet template at www.jennienash. com/blueprint.

TAKE ACTION

- Begin your research with books. Go to the bookstore and plant yourself in front of the section where you hope your book will be shelved. Look at books like yours—ones you admire, ones that you think look good in terms of how they are packaged and presented. Look in the acknowledgement section and see if an agent is mentioned. Note these names on your spreadsheet. Before you leave the bookstore, be sure to buy a book or two so that the bookstore will be there the next time you need it.

- Continue your research at home with the books on your shelf that are similar to the one you are writing and the books you identified as comp titles. Google the author and "literary agent" to see what you can turn up.

- Google the agents on your list. Visit their websites. You are looking for agents who represent books like yours, who are open to receiving queries at this time, and who you feel would be a good match for you. Click through to any podcasts the agent has done, or interviews, or guest posts, so you can get a feel for their work and their philosophy. What kind of vibe do you get? Does this agency look like "home" to you? Finding a good agent match is far more of an art than a science.

- If you have friends who are agented writers, who have either offered to introduce you to their agent or who you would like to ask for that favor, make sure the agent is a good fit before making this move. You can embarrass your friend or yourself if you don't do your homework. If someone you know can introduce you to an agent who is a good fit, I believe the best thing to do is to show the friend your finished proposal; this proves how serious you are about your book and gives them a chance to see exactly what the agent will see. If the friend is comfortable with what you have developed, ask if they will send your proposal to the agent or make you an introduction so that you can send it yourself.

- When you find an agent who is a good match, note on your spreadsheet the name of the agency, what the agent requests in a submission, which books they represent that are similar to yours, and something personal that connects you to this agent (e.g., they represent your favorite author, they are looking for the exact sort of book you have written, they say things in an interview that speak to you). You want to have some reason why you chose this agent, because you will be telling them this reason in your query letter. Just saying, "I think it would be cool to be represented by the same agent who represents Malcolm Gladwell" is not enough.

> **PRO TIP:** *You need to note the submission require-*
> *ments because you need to do exactly what they say.*
> *Many agents reject queries because very simple rules*
> *were not followed. They get too many queries to make*
> *exceptions to their requirements. Some agents ask*
> *that you do not attach any materials to the email, for*
> *example, but paste in all required elements. Others*
> *want a PDF. Agents take these rules seriously. Your job*
> *is to do the same.*

- Find agents in online agent databases. Use keywords (e.g., your category or book topic) to hunt for additional agents who would be suitable to pitch. These are some popular places to search:
  - » Agent Query – www.agentquery.com
  - » Agent Tracker – www.agenttracker.com
  - » Manuscript Wish List – www.manuscriptwishlist.com
  - » Publisher's Marketplace – www.publishersmarketplace.com
  - » Reedsy – www.reedsy.com
  - » Twitter – There are a lot of agents on Twitter, and they frequently post when they are open and closed to new queries, what they are looking for, and where they will be doing any "speed dating" events online or at conferences.

....
Make a Pitch Strategy

O nce you have a list of agents, you might be tempted to send out all 30 query letters at one time and see what sticks, but this method of pitching robs you of the chance to learn while you go. Remember that once you query an agent for a book, that's *it*. You can't go back later and say you made your proposal better. Unless they invite you to revise and resubmit, all you can do is cross them off your list and move on. You want to make the most of every query you send.

It is equally misguided to send one query at a time and wait to hear back from that agent. This method could take years.

A better strategy is the batch method of pitching where you rank the agents and pitch to a handful at a time with personalized letters. Batching your queries allows you to adjust and pivot, if you need to. It allows you to incorporate what you learn from the kinds of reactions you receive.

- If your first batch of queries gets no personal response of any kind—you either hear nothing, or you receive nothing but form letters (you've seen enough of these in your life; you know what they sound like even when they are kind)—you can assume something is off with your query.

- If your query elicits the request for more materials, you know that your query is working.

- If you received polite rejections on the requested materials, this tells you that something is off with the material you are sending.

- If you receive personal rejections on the requested material—agents indicating that they spent time with the material and actually considered your proposal but for some reason don't feel the project is a good fit for them—you know you are on the right track and can confidently keep pitching.

The Batch Method

Here's how the batch method works:

1. Rank your agents into three groups—Tier 1 are your favorites and Tier 3 are your least favorites; Tier 2 agents fall in the middle. Remember that all these agents are a good fit for your project and can serve you in the way you wish to be served, so this is a somewhat arbitrary ranking. That being said, most writers have no problem selecting their favorites.

2. Start by pitching the agents at the top of Tier 1. This is a risky strategy to be sure, but it makes good sense. If you start with your *least* desirable agents and get an offer, you might never get a chance at your top choices. You can't tell an agent to wait a month or so while you pitch someone else and see if you can get

a better offer; that would be rude, and a terrible way to start a business partnership. You generally have to say yes or no to the offer of representation within a few days, unless there are other agents actively considering the work. In that case, you could take a week or so, and you would tell all involved agents that you are weighing several offers of representation. So start with your favorite agents—and make sure you have all your pitch materials in great shape before you pitch.

PRO TIP: *If you have a personal introduction to an agent and they are in your top tier, you might consider sending them the proposal on an exclusive basis before you pitch to anyone else. It can take time to wait to hear back from them, but it is akin extending a professional courtesy to them. Just be sure that if they say yes, you would be thrilled with the match.*

3. It's best to query in small batches—I suggest five or six at a time—in case you get feedback that suggests you might want to make some revisions in your pitch or proposal.

4. Send out a new batch every two or three weeks.

TAKE ACTION

- Rank the agents on your list.
- Arrange your spreadsheet to reflect the three tiers.
- Continue to pay attention to agent news on Twitter and elsewhere and add or subtract agents to your list based on what you learn.

Write a Query Letter

Before sending your book proposal to an agent you'll send a short pitch called a query letter. The main goal of the query letter is to get the agent to request additional materials from the proposal. You can use material from your book jacket, your point, your audience analysis, and your overview to craft a query letter; you've got everything you need from the work you've done on the *Blueprint* and book proposal.

Many agents receive hundreds of queries *every week*. They evaluate them very quickly and dismiss them even faster. You need a professional query letter to stand out. It should be properly formatted, between 250 and 400 words, and written in first person. It should include these elements:

1. Open with one stellar sentence that poses a question, sets a hook, and gives a bit of dramatic context. You want something that will grab the reader by the throat and refuse to let go. You may already have this sentence written in your overview or book jacket copy.

2. Follow the hook with a short paragraph that gives the entire essence of the book. It tells the agent who this book is for—so something about the reader's pain

and their desire. It states what the reader will come to learn or understand or master—so something about the reader transformation journey and the outcome you are promising.

3. Provide an explanation of who you are and why you are writing this book. This is a very short version of your author bio. Think two, or perhaps, three lines.

4. State the estimated word count of your book. For example: "Upon completion, this book will be 72,000 words."

5. Highlight one or two comparable titles if it helps the agent place it in context. This is often a *very small* part of the query, but still an important one.

6. Express why you chose the agent. Write something personal about this particular agent that shares why you think they might be a good fit. The personalized part of a query should be no more than two or three lines. This can be very personal (e.g., they represent a book you love or an author you love). It can be the fact that you heard them speak or met them at a conference. It can even be that they love to garden or went to the same college as you. If there is nothing specific to say—if nothing jumps out at you that warrants a personalization—it's okay to leave it out. It's better to skip it than to force it.

Take your time in writing your query letter. It often takes multiple revisions to write an excellent one, and excellence always pays off in a pitch.

Online Forms

Some agents use online submission forms for their queries. They ask you to fill in the blanks, and sometimes the material they ask for doesn't exactly match the materials you have prepared. They might, for example, ask you to submit a 250-word "book jacket copy" instead of a query letter or a "summary" instead of an overview. What should you do? Don't get hung up on the language; think about what the agent is asking for and why.

- Book jacket copy focuses on the book itself without all the other elements of a query letter. Trim your material to fit the request.

- A summary and an overview are likely the same thing.

- If someone is asking for 10 pages of the proposal, you'll have to pick and choose which elements best represent your book.

- If someone is asking for 10 pages of the manuscript, you probably want to submit the first 10 pages of the introduction or Chapter 1.

CASE STUDY #1

Query Letter for *Happy Campers: Happy Campers: 9 Summer Camp Secrets for Raising Kids Who Become Thriving Adults* by Audrey Monke

Note that Audrey pitched her book with a different subtitle than the one that ended up on the published book.

"Happy camper" is not just a glib idiom. For many children, summer camp is their "happy place" where they feel more valued, connected, comfortable, and relaxed than they do the rest of the year. In formal research I conducted while receiving a master's degree in psychology, I proved that kids really are happier at camp—a truth I knew in my heart from three decades running one of the nation's top summer sleep-away camps. In *Happy Campers: Parenting Secrets from 30 Years of Summer Camp* I share behind-the-scenes stories from my work with thousands of campers and their parents, research about why campers actually *are* happier at camp, and specific ways parents can bring some of the "magic" of summer camp home.

The overarching reason for the transformational changes campers experience at summer camp in just a few weeks is not, in fact, the fresh air and fun. It is the positive culture that is intentionally created through very specific, planned practices and traditions honed over years of research and experimentation. The ten secrets of summer camp I share in this book can help parents create a happier, more connected family culture where kids thrive. The research (mine and the experts on whose shoulders I stand) proves that we can change our kids' lives by changing their environment—whether at summer camp or home.

I have developed a formal proposal for *Happy Campers*, as well as three polished sample chapters. The manuscript will be complete by Oct. 1, 2017. I am seeking representation and believe you would be an excellent fit because of your track record for sharing new and much-needed parenting ideas.

I graduated from Stanford University in 1988 and purchased Gold Arrow Camp in 1989. While researching and developing trainings for our counselors and working with thousands of campers and parents for the last 30 years,

I have learned important techniques for creating positive changes in kids. In 2010, I began sharing ideas with camp professionals by becoming a regular contributor to *Camping Magazine*, the American Camp Association's Camp Parents blog, and other camp-related sites. In 2012, I started my Sunshine Parenting website, where I write about camp, parenting, and lessons from positive psychology. I have a loyal following of parents and camp professionals, and have also developed professional relationships with prominent parenting and psychology experts, including Tina Payne Bryson (author of *The Whole-Brain Child*), who is a summer camp proponent, and my friend Christine Carter (author of *Raising Happiness* and *The Sweet Spot*) who is a Gold Arrow Camp parent and a supporter of my work.

Thank you for your consideration. I look forward to hearing from you.

Sincerely,

Audrey Monke

CASE STUDY #2
Query Letter for *Braided: A Journey of Thousand Challahs* by Beth Ricanati, MD

Note that Beth pitched her book with a different title than the one that ended up on the published book.

Five years ago, I was like every other stressed out multitasking working mom in America. I believed that I had reached my goal of walking 10,000 steps a day if I ran in place in my bathroom late at night, sorting the mail. Ironically, I was the medical director of the Cleveland Clinic's Wellness Institute's Lifestyle180 program. I was not only supposed to know better, I was supposed to *inspire* better, because the medical community is very clear that stress doesn't just make you metaphorically sick. Stress makes you actually sick.

It took me 10 years and a thousand challahs to make a change toward health and peace in my own life. *Make Challah and Call Me in the Morning: A Physician's Simple Recipe for Healthy Living* is part memoir, part cookbook and part manifesto. It is my story, and a recipe for how other women can stop and smell the rising yeast.

After 15 years as clinical doctor, I am now working as a medical consultant to several medical companies, including YouBeauty.com, where I also write a column on everyday wellness. I have been a guest contributor for television, print and online media, have published medical articles in peer-reviewed journals, and have been quoted frequently in the media on the subject of women's wellness. At the Cleveland Clinic, I worked for Mike Roizen, co-author with Mehmet Oz of the *You* books on wellness, and he will be a vocal supporter of my publishing effort—including, I hope, contributing a foreword.

I am pleased to offer you this project on an exclusive basis. Wendy Mogel's work has been such an inspiration to me; in particular, we turned again and again to *The Blessing of a Skinned Knee* when raising our young children. Jennie has been singing your praises, too, and I am hoping you believe that we might be a good fit. The manuscript is complete at 42,000 words. Please find herein a complete proposal and sample chapters for your consideration.

Sincerely,
Beth Ricanati

TAKE ACTION

- Write a query letter template following the key steps. Make sure it includes the key components:
  - » Opening hook
  - » Explanation of reader pain and reader transformation journey
  - » Short author bio
  - » Word count
  - » Comp titles if appropriate
  - » Why you chose the agent
- Revise and polish the letter.
- Personalize each query for each agent.

....

Pitch!

I t's time to pitch! After all the work you've done, all that's left to do it press a button!

Agents may reply anywhere from a minute later (I have seen this happen twice in my career) to never (it happens all the time), so expect all possibilities.

If an agent expresses interest in your work, try to stay calm and remember that the author-agent relationship is first and foremost a business relationship. You might feel an upswell of love for this person who has expressed love for your work, and that is entirely natural, but before you leap into an agreement, you need to come back to earth and ask the agent some tough questions. Consider the following:

Questions About the Project

- **What do you think of my project?** This may seem like an obvious question, but it's not. You want to hear the enthusiasm in their voice and to know exactly what they responded to in the work.

- **What is your vision for my book?** How do they see the book existing in the world?

- **Do you believe my proposal needs editing?** You want a clear idea of how much work the agent expects you to do before pitching to editors. Some agents may want you to do a few tweaks that might take a week or two. Others may have a bigger overhaul in mind. If an overhaul is proposed, make sure you agree with the direction and ask why they want you to change it. Only agree to make changes you are happy about.

- **Are you offering representation now or not until I make the proposed changes?** Doing revisions on spec is known as an R&R—revise and resubmit. It is a risk for the writer because you can do all that work and the agent might still say no, so make sure you understand what is being asked of you and what is being promised.

Questions About the Relationship

- **What would your ideal client look like, and what would your nightmare client look like?** It can be helpful to get a sense of the agent's working style. How do they like their clients to communicate? What irritates them?

- **What is your vision for my career?** If you are interested in writing more than one book, you want to know what the agent's vision for your career might be. How do they see you in 5 or 10 years? What role do they wish to play in your career?

Questions About Offers of Representation

- **When will you send your contract and when do you want me to return it?**

- **When do you expect to send the proposal out on submission? Who do you plan to send it to?**

- **What is your process during submission?** Will they update you about every manuscript request, rejection, and offer, or will they only let you know about publisher offers?

TAKE ACTION

- Send queries to the agents in the first tier of your agent spreadsheet.

- Track the requests to send more material, and note the rejections.

- If an agent asks for a partial or full proposal, send the items they request within 24 hours.

- If you get form letter rejections, evaluate them. If you get personal notes, determine if there is any information in the letters you can use to strengthen your pitch.

- After two or three weeks have passed, if you haven't heard from any agents, send out another batch. Continue sending out batches of queries. Research additional agents and add to your list.

- If an agent offers to represent your book and you feel that they would be a good business partner, celebrate your achievement! It's a big deal and you've worked hard for it!

- After the celebration, let any other agent who has requested material know so that they can make an offer if they wish.

- Interview each agent and make a decision. Let the other agents know that you have decided to sign with someone else.

Pitching Small Publishers, Academic Presses, or Hybrid Publishers

The pitch process for small publishers, academic presses, and hybrid publishers proceeds in a very similar way to the framework I have just laid out for pitching to traditional publishers.

TAKE ACTION

- Research small publishers, academic presses, or hybrid publishers that represent books similar to yours.

- Identify those accepting submissions.

- Create a spreadsheet to track their requirements and rank them according to best fit—again, this is more art than science; listen to your instincts.

- Write a query template, and then personalize it for each publisher.

- Send your queries to the first five or so on your list. Follow the batch method as responses come in.

- Respond to requests for more information within 24 hours.

- If they offer to publish your book, ask the same questions you would ask an agent: what appeals to them, what support will they provide, how do they see your book in the world as part of their universe, what is their contract and submission process?

Conclusion

I've had the pleasure and the privilege of guiding hundreds of writers and book coaches through the *Blueprint*, the book proposal development process, and pitching. It's been an exhilarating ride! One of the most surprising things I've learned is that the deepest satisfaction people end up feeling has little to do with the outcome everyone starts out seeking—the book deal, the big public impact. What moves people the most is the pride they feel in doing the thing they always wanted to do. Writing books is about words and ideas, to be sure, and it's about money and prestige, but it also has a very personal component. When you write a book, you are raising your voice, spreading the messages you believe in the most, and claiming your power.

It's life-changing work and I wish you the best of luck with it.

PRO TIP: *Turn to the next section to learn about* Blueprint *courses and* Blueprint *coaching.*

Resources: Where to Learn More

Take an online course

Learn about the course offerings at www.jennienash.com/blueprint.

Work with an Author Accelerator Certified Book Coach

Working with a book coach before you start to write is the single best investment you can make in your book. It will save you so much time and most writers end up loving the experience. My book coach certification program at Author Accelerator trains coaches in the *Blueprint for a Book* system, nonfiction book proposal development, and pitching. We have certified more than 100 book coaches, and we provide a matching service that pairs writers with a coach who is a great fit for their project. Go to www.authoraccelerator.com to learn more.

Note that for the purposes of clarity, I combined certain steps of the *Blueprint* in this book and presented them in a slightly different order than we teach in our courses. If you work with one of our coaches, the steps may look slightly different. It's all the same thing—and each coach adds their own genius to the mix. Please do not hold on too tightly to the number of steps or the order.

Become a Book Coach Yourself

The Author Accelerator book coach certification program teaches you how to coach nonfiction writers through the entire book development process. The *Blueprint for a Book* system is central to the course experience. Check out our certification program at www.bookcoaches.com/abc. We would be delighted to have you join our community of coaches.

Notes

Introduction

- Sara Ross's book is *Dear Work: I Love You, But Something Has to Change* (Page Two Books, 2023). Her website is www.sarajross.com. The poem Sara loves is "Autobiography in Five Short Chapters" by Portia Nelson from the book, *There's a Hole in My Sidewalk: The Romance of Self-Discovery*

- Michael Bungay Stanier very generously shares inside information about all his books. I frequently share the link to his story about his selling of *The Coaching Habit: Say Less, Ask More & Change the Way You Lead Forever* (Page Two Books, November 16, 2019), where he talks about his decision to publish with a hybrid publisher and what he makes per book. The article is now out of date in terms of how many books he's sold, but it's very informative about process. You can find that article here: www.linkedin.com/pulse/exactly-how-i-self-published-my-book-sold-180000-bungay-stanier. The information about Stanier's most recent book sales comes from here: www.careynieuwhof.com/episode474/

- The statistic about 2020 book sales comes from this article in *The New York Times*: www.nytimes.com/2021/04/18/books/book-sales-publishing-pandemic-coronavirus.html

- Jane Friedman's quote comes from this 2021 blog post. Jane is one of the industry's leaders on the future of publishing and publishing as a business: www.janefriedman.com/how-much-do-authors-earn

- My client Jenn Lim, author of *Beyond Happiness: How Authentic Leaders Prioritize Purpose and People for Growth and Impact* (Grand Central Publishing, October 21, 2021), introduced me to the idea of what she calls "The Other ROI" when I was coaching her on this book. The impact we make on our teams, our communities, and our planet when we are aligned with our values at work is a core tenant of what she teaches.

Blueprint Step #1:
Why Write This Book?

- I turn to a lot of business books to learn how to better help writers. Simon Sinek's *Start With Why: How Great Leaders Inspire Everyone to Take Action)* is one I go back to again and again.

- Dr. Jennifer Noble's answer is from her *Blueprint*. Her book, entitled *Secrets from the Other Side of the Tracks: What Poor Minority Kids Can Teach Your Kids About Changing the World* was a work in progress at the time of this book's publication. Her website is www.drjenntherapy.com.

- Andrea Jarrell's answer is from her *Blueprint*. Her book, entitled *Ambitious Aging: How I Learned to Think Big About My Next 50 Years* was a work in progress at the time of this book's publication. Her website is www.andrea-jarrell.com.

Blueprint Step #2:
Why Am I the Best Person to Write This Book?

- Michael Melcher's answer is from his *Blueprint*. His book is entitled *Your Invisible Network: How to Create, Maintain, and Leverage the Relationships That Will Transform Your Career* (Matt Holt Books, imprint of BenBella Books, 2023). His website is www.michaelmelcher.com.

- Becky Vieira's answer is from her *Blueprint*. Her book is entitled *The Baby Will Be Just Fine: The (Not So) Selfish Mom's Guide to Surviving the First Year* (Union Square & C, 2023). Her Instagram is @wittyotter.

Blueprint Step #5:
Choose a Working Title

- I'm a big fan of Guy Raz's podcast, How I Built This. I learn so much about creativity and productivity and just being a human in the world. The Jay Shetty episode is: hibtjayshetty.nprpresents.org.

- I learned about the story of *Skinny Bitch: A No-Nonsense, Tough-Love Guide for Savvy Girls Who Want To Stop Eating Crap and Start Looking Fabulous!* by Rory Freedman and Kim Barnouin (Running Press Adult,

December 27, 2005) here: www.bizjournals.com/
bizwomen/news/profiles-strategies/2015/04/their-
big-break-came-when-victoria-beckham-walked.
html?page=all

- I've followed Rachel Rodgers for years. She's very inspiring, and a model of how to stay focused on an ideal audience. I highly recommend her book, *We Should All Be Millionaires: A Woman's Guide to Earning More, Building Wealth, and Gaining Economic Power* (HarperCollins Leadership, May 4, 2021).

- Becky Vieira's title brainstorm is from her *Blueprint*.

- Dr. Jennifer Noble's title brainstorm is from her *Blueprint*.

Blueprint Step #6:
Who is Your Ideal Reader?

- Pam Slim coached me on my business at a critical crossroads. She is so wise and generous. Her book, *The Widest Net: Unlock Untapped Markets and Discover New Customers Right in Front of You* (McGraw Hill, November 9, 2021), is a fantastic guide to how to market anything, including books.

- The Brené Brown podcast with Emily Nagoski and Amelia Nagoski, authors of *Burnout: The Secret to Unlocking the Stress Cycle* (Ballantine Books, January 7, 2020) can be found here: https://brenebrown.com/podcast/brene-with-emily-and-amelia-nagoski-on-burnout-and-how-to-complete-the-stress-cycle

- Jennifer Noble's ideal reader description is from her *Blueprint.*

Blueprint Step #7:
What Transformation Are You Promising?

- Karen Hugg's transformation journey is from her *Blueprint.* Her book is entitled, *Leaf Your Troubles Behind: How to Destress and Grow Happiness through Plants* (Prometheus, July 15, 2022). Her website is www.karenhugg.com. Karen was coached by Author Accelerator Certified Coach Gretel Hakanson. Her website is: www.gretelhakanson.com.

Blueprint Step #8:
What Other Books Speak to Your Ideal Reader?

- Michael Bungay Stanier, author of *The Coaching Habit: Say Less, Ask More & Change the Way You Lead Forever,* often compares his book to artist Austin Kleon's *Steal Like an Artist: 10 Things Nobody Told You About Being Creative* (Workman Publishing Company, February 28, 2012). You can see one such mention here: growthlab.com/how-to-self-publish-a-book-and-double-revenue/#part-5

- Quote from *Made to Stick: Why Some Ideas Survive and Others Die* by Chip Dan Heath (Random House, January 2, 2007).

- Dr. Beth Ricanati's ideal reader description is from her *Blueprint.* Her book is *Braided: A Journey of a Thousand Challahs* (She Writes Press, September 18, 2018). Her website is www.bethricanatimd.com.

- Audrey Monke's ideal reader description is from her *Blueprint.* Her book is *Happy Campers: 9 Summer Camp Secrets for Raising Kids Who Become Thriving Adults* (Center Street, May 7, 2019). Her website is www.sunshine-parenting.com.

Blueprint Step #12:
Design a Table of Contents

- *Cooked: A Natural History of Transformation* by Michael Pollan (Penguin Press, April 23, 2013). Pollan's books all have fantastic tables of contents.

- *The Top Five Regrets of the Dying: A Life Transformed by the Dearly Departing* by Bronnie Ware (Hay House Inc., March 20, 2012).

- *Why Design Matters: Conversations with the World's Most Creative People* by Debbie Millman Harper Design (February 22, 2022). The anecdote is from *Fast Company* article: www.fastcompany.com/90723094/in-a-new-anthology-debbie-millman-distills-17-years-of-conversations-about-design-and-creativity?partner=rss&utm_source=twitter.com&utm_medium=social&utm_campaign=rss+fastcompany&utm_content=rss

- Gretchen Rubin's quote is from an interview she and I had on December 20, 2021.

- Table of Contents from *The Five Love Languages: How to Express Heartfelt Commitment to your Mate* (Northfield Publishing, January 1, 1992) by Dr. Gary Chapman. Permission granted from Moody Publishers, Moodypublishers.com, December 30, 2021.

- Table of Contents from *The Artist's Way: A Spiritual Path to Higher Creativity* by Julie Cameron (Tarcher, January 1, 1992). Permission granted by Penguin Random House LLC, date January 7, 2022.

Blueprint Step #13:
Create an Outcome Outline

- Susanne Dunlap's Outcome Outline is from her *Blueprint*. Her book, *Compose Yourself: The Essential History of Musical Women Who Broke the Silence and Dazzled Their World,* was a work in progress at the time of this book's publication. Her website is susannedunlap.com. She was coached by Author Accelerator Certified Coach Barbara Boyd. Her website is www.barbarajboyd.com

- Dan Blank's Outcome Outline is from his *Blueprint*. His book, *Share Like It Matters,* was a work in progress at the time of this book's publication. His website is www.wegrowmedia.com.

Blueprint Step #14:
Write Book Jacket Copy

- Book jacket copy is from *The Next Happy: Let Go of the Life You Planned and Find a New Way Forward* by Tracy Cleantis (Hazelden Publishing, January 29, 2015), now known as Tracy Cleantis Dwyer. Her website is www.traceyhappy.com.

- Book jacket copy is from *The Divorce Hacker's Guide to Untying the Knot: What Every Woman Needs to Know about Finances, Child Custody, Lawyers, and Planning*

Ahead by Ann E. Grant (New World Library, October 2, 2018). Her website is www.thedivorcehacker.com.

Proposal Element #4:
Audience Analysis

- The sales numbers for *Atlas of the Heart: Mapping Meaningful Connection and the Language of Human Experience* (Random House, November 30, 2021), by Brené Brown and *Miss Independent: A Simple 12-Step Plan to Start Investing and Grow Your Own Wealth* by Nicole Lapin (HarperCollins Leadership (February 1, 2022) came from this article: www.publishersweekly.com/pw/nielsen/HardcoverNonfiction.html.

- The Steve Laube quote comes from here: https://stevelaube.com/what-are-average-book-sales. His website is www.stevelaube.com.

Acknowledgements

Thanks to all my Author Accelerator book coaches and to Laura Franzini, our COO, for pushing me to clarify and explain everything about *Blueprint for a Nonfiction Book* and the Outcome Outline. These tools are better because of the scrutiny and the iterations.

Thanks to Author Accelerator certified coach Barbara Boyd for coaching me through the dark night of the soul on this book and towards a much better book in every way; the experience was a perfect example of the power of working with a book coach!

Thanks to Author Accelerator certified book coach Leslie H. Cole for your careful proofreading.

Thanks to all the writers who have let me coach you with these tools, and to the writers who allowed me to share their work: Dan Blank, Tracey Cleantis Dwyer, Michelle Dempsey-Multack, Susanne Dunlap (*Blueprint* and proposal coached by Author Accelerator certified book coach Barbara Boyd), Ann Grant, Renee Guilbault, Karen Hugg (*Blueprint* and proposal coached by Author Accelerator certified book coach Gretel Hakanson), Andrea Jarrell, Michael Melcher, Audrey Monke, Dr. Jennifer Noble, Dr. Beth Ricanati, and Becky Vieira.

Thanks to Carla Green of Clarity Designworks for the interior layout; and Stuart Bache for the cover.

Thanks to Lianne Scott for backing me up every day so I can write and think and coach.

Thanks to Rob, Carlyn, and Emily once again and always for cheering me on.

About the Author

Jennie Nash is the founder and CEO of Author Accelerator, a company that certified and supports book coaches so they can teach and support writers. She is the creator of the Author Accelerator Book Coach Certification Program and has taught hundreds of book coaches and thousands of writers how to use the *Blueprint for a Book* system to help them produce their best work in the most efficient way. Her own coaching clients have landed top New York agents; won six-figure book deals with Big Five houses such as Penguin, Scribner, Simon & Schuster, and Hachette; and landed on the *New York Times* and *Wall Street Journal* bestseller lists. Jennie is the author of 11 books in three genres, including *Blueprint for a Book: Build Your Novel from the Inside Out* and *Read Books All Day and Get Paid for It: The Business of Book Coaching.*

Visit her at www.jennienash.com (website), @jennienash (Twitter), @jennienash (LinkedIn), and @jennienashbook coach (Instagram).

Made in the USA
Middletown, DE
09 May 2023

30304587R00144